PENG

I AM

Anita Selzer

One boy's extraordinary experience of wartime survival . . .

One mother's incredible courage . . .

It is German-occupied Poland in 1942 and Jewish lives are at risk. Nazi soldiers order young boys to pull down their trousers to see if they are circumcised. Many are summarily shot or sent to the camps.

A remarkable mother takes an ingenious step. To avoid suspicion, she trains her teenage son to be a girl: his clothing, voice, hair, manners and more. Together, mother and son face incredible odds as their story sweeps backwards and forwards across occupied Europe.

'A compelling reminder of the cruelty of discrimination . . . and a testament to a boy's bravery, sublimating his true identity in the face of ever-present danger.'
SIMON FRENCH

'An astonishing story of survival set against the backdrop of the Holocaust.'
MARK BAKER, ASSOCIATE PROFESSOR OF HOLOCAUST AND GENOCIDE STUDIES, MONASH UNIVERSITY

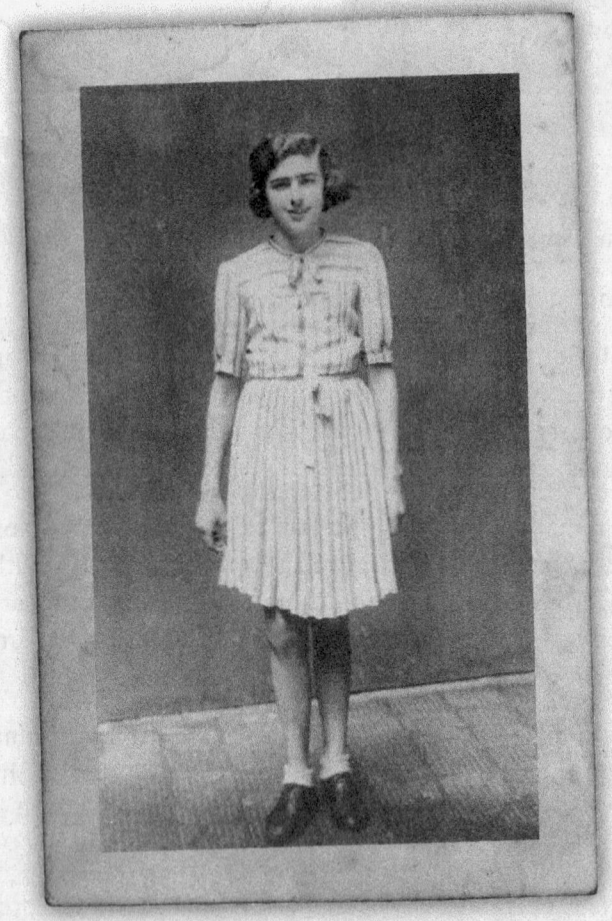

I AM SASHA
Anita Selzer

PENGUIN BOOKS

PENGUIN BOOKS

UK | USA | Canada | Ireland | Australia
India | New Zealand | South Africa | China

Penguin Books is part of the Penguin Random House group of companies whose addresses can be found at global.penguinrandomhouse.com.

First published by Penguin Random House Australia Pty Ltd, 2018

3 5 7 9 10 8 6 4

Text copyright © Anita Selzer, 2018
The moral right of the author has been asserted.

All rights reserved. Without limiting the rights under copyright reserved above, no part of this publication may be reproduced, stored in or introduced into a retrieval system, or transmitted, in any form or by any means (electronic, mechanical, photocopying, recording or otherwise), without the prior written permission of both the copyright owner and the above publisher of this book.

Design by Tony Palmer © Penguin Random House Australia Pty Ltd
Cover photographs author's own. *Back cover:* Young Sasha as a boy, before the war; the Brody ghetto; Larissa and Sasha aged around six.
Front cover: Sasha as a girl, aged fourteen and a half, July 1944.
Photograph insert: photographs from author's personal collection.
Every effort has been made to contact the copyright holders of material in this book.
Please contact the publisher with any queries.
Printed and bound in Australia by Griffin Press, an accredited ISO AS/NZS 14001
Environmental Management Systems printer

 A catalogue record for this book is available from the National Library of Australia

ISBN 978 0 1437 8574 3

penguin.com.au

*For my family,
and in memory of my wonderful father and
grandmother for their love, fortitude and resilience,
and my beloved mother who sadly passed away
not having the chance to read this book.*

AUTHOR'S NOTE

Sasha's tale is based upon a true story, originally written down by Sasha's mother, Larissa, in her memoir, but all names have been changed. It is a tribute to all the survivors of the war – and to all those who did not come home. Sasha was actually my father and Larissa my grandmother. This is their story.

CONTENTS

Prologue 1

PART ONE	The Boy 5
Chapter 1	Cafe Days 6
Chapter 2	Shadows Gather 18
Chapter 3	War Strikes 35
Chapter 4	Bella Kowalski 55
Chapter 5	Flight 69
Chapter 6	The Barn 86
PART TWO	The Girl 103
Chapter 7	Zayda 104
Chapter 8	Desperate Measures 114
Chapter 9	How to be a Girl 125
Chapter 10	Back to Lwów 138
Chapter 11	Sala Steps Out 152
Chapter 12	The Real Girls in My Life 163
Chapter 13	Eva 176
Chapter 14	Zegota 193
Chapter 15	The Landscape of War 211

PART THREE	And Me 223
Chapter 16	Sala is Gone 224
Chapter 17	Life in Gliwice 235
Chapter 18	Displacement 253
Chapter 19	Munich – and Mila 266
Chapter 20	A New Land 287
Chapter 21	Coming Home 298
	The Story Behind the Story 311
	Timeline 317
	Glossary 321
	Acknowledgements 325
	About the Author 327

PROLOGUE

Fremantle, Australia – March 1950

It is a hot summer's day. The name of our boat is the *Surriento*. She drops her anchor and surrenders us to the sweltering Australian sun, my first experience of such heat. I hear Mama and others who've travelled with us talking about America, and of British and Dutch submarines, and I think it's strange that the war, my war, has touched even places as far away and unimaginable for me as this.

But after only a few minutes the heat starts to get to me, and I return to our cabin and lie on the lower bunk, just below the waterline. I can see the grey-green water lap against our one porthole. I try to sleep, but only doze, and I can hear all the commotion outside on the upper decks, people hurrying around, wanting to get outside and see their new country. I just want some quiet away from everyone else.

I lie here and think of home, of Poland and my beautiful town of Lwów. There are times when I cannot tell if I'm dreaming or if I'm awake.

I remember so many things. But there's one day that haunts me still, whether I'm awake or asleep.

It was a day when Mama and I were hiding in a barn. There were shots, and terrible cries, and I was pleading with her. 'Mama, I don't want to die! *Do* something!' I screamed as bombs exploded outside, and many shots were fired. Cries followed – men, women and children. And then the silence. I remember peering through the window and saw a German soldier slapping an old man. Another pointed a gun to a boy's head. 'Pull down your trousers!' he shouted. The boy was circumcised, so the soldier pulled the trigger and I saw blood splatter in the street. 'Dirty Jew!' the soldier spat.

And then the door of the barn burst open . . .

I lie still on my bunk and think of this day, so long ago now. How do you try and forget things that change your life forever? Can you?

I think of our old home in Poland. I see the details of our apartment in Lwów, the walnut timber bedheads, the plasterwork round the ceiling – I remember sobbing on my bed for ages one day, crying and yelling at Mama, 'I can't do it! You want too much, Mama!' My heart thumps harder just thinking about it. I was thirteen then, and so confused. And I got up and stood in front of the mirror in the door of my wardrobe. I just stand there and I look at my dress, which I hate – it has stripes and I hate stripes, and the hem is uneven and I don't even have a proper waist like a girl should have. And the dress feels like it's choking me because the collar is one of those ones with a tie ribbon at the front and buttons that do up high to the neck. It's very uncomfortable. Mama just says I should stop complaining and think how lucky I am to have a dress like this at all.

I start to stroke my hair down flat on top of my head. I hate my hair too – I liked it better before I let it grow. Now it's all curly and it sticks out at the sides and it's not even pretty like girls' hair should be. I hate this so much! Everything, my shoes, my socks, even the way I stand . . .

Then I imagine again the sound of bombs dropping and suddenly I am fully awake, because Mama has come down to the cabin to get me.

'You were thinking again, weren't you?' she says quietly.

'Yes. Just daydreaming.'

'About?'

'Home. Just home.'

'But darling, out *there* is home now!' She points to the porthole and the waves lapping at the edges. 'Your new country, *our* new country. Australia! It will be all right. Come on up and join the others.'

So I do as Mama says and go back up outside. But

all the time I can't help thinking about me, standing in front of that mirror. And I can't help thinking of this story I have that I really need to tell someone. To tell you and everyone.

So in the next pages that's what I'll try to do. Tell the story of a boy I once knew. Actually, I will let him tell you the story himself.

For this we have to go a long, long way from here, back again to Poland . . .

PART ONE
THE BOY

Chapter 1
CAFE DAYS

My story begins in Schwabendorf, on the outskirts of Brody, a small pretty town near the Styr River, where lots of Jewish people like my family lived, and where I was born in 1929. I used to call it Schwaby. It's weird, what I remember, and how far back I can go in my head.

I only have really faint memories of when I was little, but I can still see myself dressed in a pale-blue sailor suit with white buttons down the front. I seem to remember it wasn't very comfortable. Mama used to take me for walks around town, through the parks and around huge statues with flowerbeds at the bottom. In winter it was pretty but icy cold. My mama would always wear a hat and often gloves. I remember the feel of the leather gloves in my hand as we walked. That's one of my very first memories of being little. Or maybe I'm just remembering a photograph Mama had of me.

I do remember Mama telling me stories, though. She was a great storyteller. She'd tell me all about Papa. He died when I was only two so I don't remember him at all really. Just photos again. But I'll never forget the screams the night he died. I remember Mama yelling. For years after that she'd say to me, 'Your father was a good man, kind and generous. Don't think of the night he died. Think of how *proud* he was of you! You were such a lovely baby, Sasha! Such blond curly hair and blue eyes! Your father was overjoyed when you were born. Every Sunday he'd take you for a walk to the park in your pram. And he loved cuddling you! It was just the three of us together then.'

I could see tears in her eyes even all these years later, whenever she talked about Papa.

'What about Zayda?' My dear grandfather. Zayda is my Yiddish name for him.

'Oh yes, he was thrilled, of course! All he ever wanted was a grandchild, a boy or a girl he could play chess with. That was his real passion in life, that game. He was happy with a grandson or a granddaughter. As long as he could teach you chess. And your beloved grandmother. We called her Bubbe . . .'

'But I don't remember Bubbe.'

'No, of course not, Sasha. Your grandmamma died long before you were born.' Mama always looked sad when she spoke of my Bubbe.

Her sadness made me feel that way too, and I thought of Papa again. I wish I could remember more of when I was very small, and of the times I spent with him. I only seem to be able to remember silly things, like the colour of my socks or the sailor hat I used to wear. Sometimes I try to force myself to think of Papa, but nothing comes into my head.

'And some days I'd take you to see your papa's mother too,' Mama would say. But I noticed that when she talked about Papa's mother she'd go all quiet and wouldn't tell me any more. I think it was something to do with Papa's mother not approving of Mama, but I didn't know about that then. I still don't really understand it. But anyway, my papa died suddenly – a heart attack – Mama said, and that's all I needed to know. And even though I didn't have much time with him, he loved me very much and I should always think of him as my papa even though I only ever knew what it was like to have my mama there with me. She'd been mother and father to me all that time.

I have to tell you that now, because it's very important in this story. I was Mama's sole responsibility and she'd always do whatever it took to protect me. 'Sasha, you are my life, my *whole* life,' she said.

The other very important thing you have to know about us is that I was born in a country where Jews had suffered a lot in the past. Mama told me about this too, about this thing called anti-Semitism, a hatred towards Jews that had been going on for centuries in Poland where we lived.

But when I was growing up all that suddenly became worse. Much worse. In 1931 when I was only about two, I think, in Lwów, where we'd eventually live, a pogrom had broken out. Our town of Lwów – you have to say it right; *Le Vov* – that's how you say it. Anyway, Jewish shops and businesses were attacked, and Jews were not only hurt in the skirmishes, but they were also killed by Polish soldiers and civilians. Killed on purpose! I couldn't imagine how people could do this, to their own people. And the Jewish area in our town was burned.

Life became even tougher for Jews after that. Sometimes I heard Mama and Zayda talk about bad times, a depression they said, that was affecting Poland, and there were lots of people who'd lost their jobs. They said the Jews had suffered the most and many were living on around fifty *zlotys* a week. I didn't really know how much that was. 'Barely enough to survive on at all!' Mama said and rolled her eyes.

Even Mama had lots of trouble finding a job when I was little. I remember being afraid when she had to go in the mornings and I used to cling to her skirt because I thought she'd leave and not come back. She used to catch a train to work because we were still living in Brody then, nearly a hundred kilometres from Lwów, in the heart of the north-east. So I used to stay with Zayda until we moved to Lwów when I was four.

'My darling, I won't be away for long *and* I will bring you back a surprise!' Mama promised me one morning before she left for work.

'What will you bring me?' I was so excited about getting a present. I hardly ever got presents, except on birthdays and other special days.

'You will see. I can't tell you or it won't be a surprise.' She kissed me and hugged me goodbye and I waited the whole day for her to come home again. When she eventually did come in the door I jumped into her arms. 'Mama, Mama! Where is my surprise?' I shouted, waving my arms in the air.

'Here it is!' She helped me tear open the bright-red wrapping paper, and my eyes widened as I saw all the treasures within.

'Trains! Different-coloured trains!' I kissed Mama and started taking them out of the box to play with right there on the floor in front of her.

But then, only a few days later, I was at a real train station about to get on a real train. I was so happy because even Mama looked excited. And it's true – I don't remember much about the actual trip, but

I remember the little things. Like me smiling at Mama and pressing my face against the glass, the smell of the wooden window frame, and crowds of people on the platform, and me watching as we pulled out of the train station and began our journey to our new home of Lwów. I think now that Mama was just happy about starting again with a new future to look forward to.

Lwów was very different from our old town of Brody. 'Sasha, this is a lovely place! You will like it here. Lwów is much more cultured, with lots of things to do. It has beautiful parks. You will love the parks! Lots of room to kick a ball around. And it has synagogues and churches and amazing buildings, and a wonderful train station.' Mama squeezed my hand.

I noticed the very grand station as soon as our train pulled in. It was huge! Mama called it Art Nouveau, and I stared at the big thick stone columns and the sculptures of people in drapes – I couldn't tell if they were men or women – standing high up above the entrance. Everything looked so big to me then.

When we were living in Lwów, sometimes Mama and I would walk down *Grodecka*, the longest street in the town, just across from the railway station. It went on for nine kilometres, past the station and the opera house. I used to skip down half the street and then run until Mama caught me. She'd be panting. 'Sasha! Sasha! For goodness sake, slow down! I can't run in these shoes! Not on the cobblestones.'

A lot of Jewish people lived in the oldest part of *Grodecka* and had businesses around there. There were shoe stores, a hairdresser, the pharmacy Mama used, and a sweets factory, which I loved. Mama would buy me my favourite sticky sweet, red and white, and I would suck on bits of it and get the sticky sugar on my hands and all over my face as well.

Famous actors and artists from the theatre loved to go to *Grodecka* for the restaurants. Mama said the Austrians had built many of the buildings in Lwów. I thought that was strange because we weren't Austrians. We were Polish Jews. 'Sasha, dear, the Austrians used to run this town. It was theirs once. But the Jewish people, we have lived here even longer, for hundreds of years . . .'

She told me stories about the Jewish people in Lwów, about the synagogues and all the different sorts of shops – tailors, tanners, silversmiths and other craftsmen who made lots of beautiful things. Mama had a small silver horse she'd bought from the silversmith once. It sat on our mantelpiece, on its own little wooden stand, and I loved its curved neck and swirling mane and tail. I thought horses were beautiful animals. The little silver horse is lost now, but I can still see it in my mind and I wonder what happened to it, in the end.

Mama knew lots about history and the people of Lwów. She told me about the Jews who went to university to study law and medicine. They must have been very smart to go to university. I thought that maybe, one day, I would try to go to university too.

In those first days when we moved to Lwów, Mama would hold me in her arms and tell me stories sometimes about what it was like in the olden days, when she was growing up. She'd stroke my hair and give me a hug. 'Do you remember, Sasha, the very first time we went for a walk with Tylda?'

Tylda was Mama's cousin and special friend. We walked all over Lwów together and I'd walk between them, holding one of Mama's hands and one of Tylda's. Sometimes they'd swing me up and down, sometimes they'd let me run on ahead and look in the shop windows. They took me everywhere, to look at Lwów's grand buildings, to dodge through the crowds outside the banks and to watch the rich people dining outside the hotels in the summer. And most importantly, they would take me to the cafes.

We used to go to one very fine cafe called *Wiedenska*, not far from the art museum. I loved the warm foamy milk that was frothed up in a little cup that Tylda would order especially for me. She'd grin and say, 'Sasha, you have froth all over your chin. You look like an old man with a white beard!' and she'd laugh and wipe the milk away.

Tylda was always happy and friendly and she'd buy me cakes and laugh with me. Mama said we got on so well because Tylda's mama and my father's mama had been sisters. I thought it was more like having an aunt to look after me, and I loved our outings into town to have breakfast or something special from the delicatessen. Tylda used to order me salami on rye. It was delicious! Even when things got bad later, I still remember how that salami tasted – salty and spicy and delicious!

Sometimes Tylda took me to the confectionery shop in the same street – Zalewski's, the 'king of chocolates'. Tylda made sure my pockets were full of his sweets by the time we left.

'Oh I can't *think* what to taste!' Tylda said. 'I might have the lemon slice in aspic...no! No, no...maybe, Sasha, the marzipan! This time I'll have the marzipan! What do you think, Sasha? What looks most tasty?'

'The chocolate! The chocolate!' I cried, and she laughed and ordered the chocolate cake especially for me.

She took a bite of the cake and smacked her lips,

which made me laugh. And the marzipan she finally decided to buy was shaped like a fish. Mama said it was an allegorical figure, but I didn't understand that then and I didn't care anyway. Tylda agreed.

'Oh, it doesn't matter what it means, Larissa! As long as it tastes good! I want to try the sun made of shelled almonds too, and the stars. Look, Sasha! Little stars with white icing!'

'Delicious,' Mama said, 'but perhaps they are for next time.' And she frowned at me and Tylda.

I loved these days at the cafes, the days when I got that warm foamy frothy milk to drink.

There was another special cafe too, the Scottish Café, and there the milk was always sprinkled with grated chocolate. The Scottish Café was famous. Writers and artists and university people came to drink and eat there. It was very small, very busy, full of cigarette smoke and buzzing with noise. Tylda, Mama and I could barely hear each other when we went there, but I loved to watch the people all around us, the men in striped suits sipping coffee and the women in beautiful clothes and hats. Tylda was like that. She always wore beautiful clothes and her brown hair would be done up neatly underneath a smart felt hat, and I remember her red lipstick and shiny gold earrings. Mama said she was beautiful, like an actress from a picture-show album.

One day we were in the Scottish Café and a man came in and waved at another man to join him at his table. Soon a whole group of men were talking loudly all at once, excited about something. And then to my surprise they began to draw on the tabletop. People in the cafe seemed amazed and began to watch.

Tylda turned to Mama. 'Larissa! Who would have thought! That's Stanislaw Ulam.'

'From a well-to-do family, I suppose,' Mama said, but she didn't sound very interested. Not like Tylda.

'Yes, but Larissa, darling, these men are the crème de la crème of mathematicians here in Lwów. There!' She nodded over towards them. 'That man smoking all the time, he's Stefan Banach. And on the left is Wladyslaw Orlicz. Banach is illegitimate, you know.' She spoke only loud enough for Mama to hear above the noise.

'Mama, what does "illy-git-imit" mean?' I asked.

Mama stopped talking and looked at Tylda.

Tylda laughed and turned to me. 'Sasha, my dear, it means when a child is born to parents who are not married to each other.' Tylda would always explain things to me very simply, and I was happy with that answer and went back to my frothy drink and watching the men draw on the tables.

Tylda quickly continued. 'Well, I don't know the *real* story – there was talk of his mother being a servant of some sort in the family, but nobody really knows. Anyway, Banach turned out to be a *brilliant* man!'

Then Mama looked more closely at the group of men. 'Look, Sasha! These men are very clever. They are working out mathematical problems and drawing them with a pencil on the table – look!'

I watched, fascinated, and wondered why they were allowed to draw on a tabletop, when I'd get into terrible trouble if Mama ever saw me doing that. No sweets for a week!

I've no idea how long our lives stayed like this. I just remember how happy I was. And how much fun Tylda was, with exciting outings with friends and chocolates in cafes and delicious food. I've no idea exactly what happened or when things changed.

Maybe it happened slowly. I don't remember. I was too young. But it seemed like one day there were visits into town and chocolate milk and cakes and remembering some of the happiest days of my life with Tylda and Mama. I must have been around five I suppose. And then the next day things just changed.

Everything changed. And then there were no more outings. Tylda left Europe with her husband to go to America, before the storm really hit.

Chapter 2
SHADOWS GATHER

By the time I started kindergarten, things were very different for us. Not just different – strange, as though something was about to happen. Something that made people nervous and afraid.

But I was so little I didn't really understand what was going on. My kindergarten was my world then. It was a small Hebrew one and I went only in the mornings. Mama said I cried and cried as if I was heartbroken the first day she left me there. I don't remember how long I cried for, but I do remember my teacher coming over and trying to make me happy again. She seemed nice, and she gave me a train to play with because Mama had told her I loved to play with trains.

I remember too the time I was very sick. Mama says it was scarlet fever. My ear hurt so much that I was taken away from kindergarten and looked after at home by Mama and my nanny, Anna. Anna had wavy blonde hair and smiled a lot. One day I was home and Mama had come back from work to find me all alone, without Anna or anyone else in the apartment. I was crying in bed and wouldn't get up.

'Sasha! Where on earth is Anna?' Mama took me in her arms, and tears began to roll down her cheeks.

'Anna is gone, Mama! She went out with a man with a big moustache. I ran after her, but she didn't want to come back. I was scared. It was cold outside. So I came back and stayed in my bed to wait for you.' I kept crying, and Mama hugged me even tighter.

I'd run out into the street after Anna that day, but it was winter and freezing cold, and I'd been barefoot in my pyjamas. I remember running across the street and trying not to slip on the frosty cobblestones. I couldn't understand why Anna would just leave. I thought the man with the big moustache must have been very important or in trouble or something to make Anna leave with him like that. Anyway, after that day I got sick. And I never saw Anna again.

That's when I needed my aunts.

Now that Anna had gone, Mama had to find someone to look after me when she was at work. She had a good idea. Perhaps her sister Binka could help.

'Remember Aunty Binka, Sasha? I'll ring her this evening. I'm sure she would love to see you!'

Binka was Mama's younger sister and when she heard what had happened she was very worried about me.

'Binka, please,' Mama begged. 'Come and live with us in Lwów. I will pay for your train ticket. I can provide for us all. I need help looking after Sasha, and you could do some cooking and cleaning, basically run the home here. You *must* come. I can't trust a stranger again. And Sasha would love to see you, his very own aunt!'

I don't know what Aunty Binka said at first, but Mama said Binka had to study and she had a friend called Frederick, and she didn't want to leave him. She was asking a lot of Aunty Binka, but she and Binka were very close and she knew somehow that Binka wouldn't let her down.

A few days later Binka had decided. She'd come and help look after me.

'Isn't it wonderful, Sasha? She'll be here next Thursday, on the five o'clock train. Oh, she is my saviour!' Then Mama suddenly remembered something. 'But I must send her some money for the train ticket straight away!' She hugged me and rushed off to make the arrangements for Binka.

It was only a few days later, though, that Mama had another phone call. It was her other younger sister, Rena.

'It is lovely news, Sasha! Aunty Rena will be coming to stay too. I'll have to buy another train ticket, and we'll have to organise another bedroom, but you'll have two aunties to look after you now. We will be so much happier! It won't be like having a nanny at all. These are your own family, our blood, Sasha, and there is nothing better than that! We are very lucky. Very lucky indeed!'

So from then on I lived in our apartment with my aunties while Mama was at work, and I loved being with Binka and Aunty Rena. Binka was always singing and she had the bluest eyes, like the ocean. I liked her singing because it seemed to cheer people up when so many adults around me seemed sad a lot of the time. And Rena was very beautiful, with light-blue eyes that often looked like they were going to cry. Both aunts looked like Mama – fair-haired with blue-grey eyes. I remember Mama said that Rena was a very sensitive young woman, which is why she left after only a few weeks to go and live with Marek, a young engineer who she loved and married. They moved into an apartment in the same building as ours, so I still saw Rena all the time.

Mama also had another sister called Mania, so all together I had three aunties. Unlike the other three sisters, she had dark hair and brown eyes. 'She got married, Sasha, to a nice man called Bolek. He's an engineer, and they are going to live in Palestine.'

'Why do they want to live in Palestine? What's wrong with Poland?' I asked.

Mama sometimes went very quiet when I asked questions like this.

'Nothing, Sasha darling. There's nothing wrong with Poland. But many people want to live in Palestine. It is hard for Jewish people here sometimes. Later you will understand. But now...' She momentarily brightened. 'Guess what we will do this Thursday?'

'What will we do, Mama?'

'Dinner at Zayda's! All of us. Your aunties are coming too. And you know how much Zayda looks forward to seeing you.'

'Oooh, Friday night in Schwaby!' I loved Friday nights at my grandfather's. It was the only time in the week when Mama really relaxed. And I loved my aunts' delicious cooking.

Zayda's real name was Richard Kohn, and he lived in a beautiful wooden house near a spring, where there was always the smell of jasmines, lilacs and roses wafting into the house – Mama said Bubbe used to call it her Garden of Eden. 'I'd walk in the garden with my mama, Sasha, holding hands and smelling the fragrance of her lovely flowers. I can almost taste the sweet crunchy apples from her orchard too!'

So it was special, going to Schwaby for Friday dinner. We'd go on the train late on a Thursday afternoon – Mama, me, Binka, Rena and her husband

Marek. Mama and my aunts would buy the food from the market there and get ready for the Sabbath. There would be all of us together. There was Zayda and his second wife, Sonia – who was Bubbe's cousin and who had a little girl called Stefanie. The dining table was draped with the same embroidered white tablecloth every time and there were white linen table napkins with red roses and silvery thread sewn around the edges: Bubbe's precious things.

Mama and her sisters would always bring these out for the Sabbath, Jewish New Year and Passover. She'd proudly show me the matching silver candlesticks, her best china, silver cutlery and crystal wine glasses. 'These are family heirlooms, you know, Sasha,' she'd say, 'handed down from my mother.' I watched while Mama and her sisters polished the candlesticks and straightened the silverware around the table. Mama said it was all about family traditions and that this was very important.

My grandfather was so much fun on the Sabbath. In those days most of the other adults around me seemed to talk in whispers, as if they didn't want me to hear what they were saying, or they tried to look cheerful when I saw they were afraid. But Zayda always joked and laughed with us, with me especially. I loved the bit where Mama, and sometimes Sonia too, would light the candle, and she'd have a candle-lighting prayer, and then Zayda would do the blessing for the wine: 'Barukh atah Adonai Eloheinu Melekh ha'olam, b'ore p'ri hagafen.'

And the best bit was that I was allowed to sip a little wine from Zayda's glass. I always had to be careful because his glass was always so full. Then he'd recite the bread blessing over the challah: 'Barukh atah Adonai Eloheinu Melekh ha'olam, ha Motsi lechem min ha'aretz.'

Mama baked her own challah that afternoon and I loved the smell of it wafting through the house. All our favourite dishes were cooked: chicken soup – *yoich* with noodles and boiled carrots – except I didn't so much like the boiled carrots. Roast chicken and babka, Jewish butter cake made with yeast and chocolate – that was my favourite. My Aunty Rena's lips got messy with the dripping chocolate, and Marek would try to wipe her face with a table napkin. I'd laugh at them and then Mama would stare at me, and I knew that meant I was in trouble.

One Friday night it was raining and I'd just finished some delicious *tzimmes*, carrots sweetened with cinnamon and brown sugar, and I was happy to sit and listen to the adults. Tonight they were the same as always, talking about things that made them frown or made them begin to weep. Zayda, who was usually cheerful, looked at me quickly and got that stern look of his in the eye. This meant there was one of his lectures coming. Tonight it turned out to be about how I should have a great belief in God.

'He is the creator of everything, Sasha, my dear! God is everywhere, at all times. The creator of all nations, not just the Jews. There is only one God for all.'

'Yes, Zayda, I know.'

'You must remember that. God will be there to guide you. In bad times you must always turn to God. I still have so much to teach you, Sasha!'

'Yes, Zayda.'

'Especially the game we love most, yes?'

Zayda had a special possession – a precious ivory and ebony chess set tucked away in a cupboard in the hall. The first time he brought it out, he carried it like it was a delicate child and placed it carefully on the table in front of me. He called his chess set 'antique'.

'What does that mean, Zayda?'

'Valuable and old, my boy,' he patted me on the back and grinned. 'As old as me. It was given to me by my father. I plan to give it to my son, your Uncle Daniel. Such a pity he cannot be here tonight.'

The pieces of the chess set lived in a heavy wooden box. Each piece snuggly fitted into its position, secured by a band of ribbon. Zayda untied each ribbon and took the white pieces out first, and then the black pieces on the right. The box itself was a very clever idea, because when Zayda turned it upside down, it was used as the chess board.

Zayda placed some pieces on the board in front of me. Then he suddenly got a glint in his eye. 'Sasha, this is a very important game. Listen carefully. It's a game about two armies – one white and the other black,' he said as he continued to place each piece on the board in careful rows.

I picked up one of the chess pieces. It was shaped like a horse with a man in a pointed hat on top. I liked horses and wanted to learn to ride a horse one day. I thought the horse piece was a beautiful figure.

'The aim, my boy, is to out-think your opponent. Very important! Plan the best attack and defence. Use your army to capture the enemy and destroy the king.'

Zayda now had my immediate attention. He sounded so excited. He began to teach me what all the pieces were called, where they sat on the board and how they moved.

'The king is the most important figure in the army. If captured, the battle is lost. And the queen is the most powerful – she can move in any direction and over many squares at once. Fancy, a woman having all that power!'

Zayda then pointed to the bishop. 'This one attacks

late in the game. You move it diagonally. Only this way, Sasha,' and he showed me how the bishop moved from the spot he placed it on the board.

'What's this funny-looking one, Zayda?' I asked, picking up the horse again.

'Ah, that's the knight. He can jump over the other pieces. He moves in a very special way.'

Zayda picked up the knight and showed me how the piece could move forward and diagonally at the same time. He then grabbed the one shaped like a castle and said it was good as an attack piece and useful to defend the king.

'But how do you move it?'

'It's called a rook, Sasha. Here, forward, back or across, just like that. And the smallest pieces . . . these are the pawns, the foot soldiers in the army, advancing on the opposition.'

That evening we played our first test match. Over the next few weeks he taught me patiently until at last one evening he said, with a twinkle in his eye, 'Come on, my boy. Now you are ready for a real battle.'

I wanted to go for Zayda's king as soon as possible – but somehow I got sidetracked and I didn't notice that I'd exposed my own king far too early. Zayda smiled and showed me what I'd done, how foolish a move I'd made. Zayda could have taken my king.

'Sasha, why did you take such a risk with your king? Precious things must be protected. I taught you better than that!'

I nodded and tried to look very serious. But from that day, I swore never to let Zayda capture my king again. Sometimes I think that maybe he just let me win sometimes. But still, the best thing was when I said, 'Checkmate!' You should've seen the look on Zayda's face when I did! But it wasn't very often. Zayda taught me well, and he was very hard to beat.

I had great respect for Zayda, not just because of the chess but because he made me want to take pride in our Jewish heritage. He'd explain about all the practices of Orthodox Judaism. And new ideas too. Zayda always said that it was important to try and be a great thinker – to think for yourself, open up your mind. 'Don't just listen to others,' he said, and then scratched his head. 'Except for your mama, of course! And, Sasha, I will teach you about a man called Moses Mendelssohn. Ah, there was a great thinker! He lived about a hundred and fifty years ago, a German Jewish philosopher from Berlin. The father of our Enlightenment!'

I looked blank but tried to follow what Zayda was saying.

'It is called *Haskalah*, Sasha, the Jewish Enlightenment. You and me, all of us, must keep our traditional

Jewish values but mix with non-Jews and enjoy a secular life as well. We are all people together!' Zayda stopped for a moment, as if he were thinking great thoughts too. He took off his glasses and polished them on his sleeve, then looked at me again and said, 'God is perfect, wise, merciful and good.'

I thought this made sense, and because I liked books and reading I wanted to find out more. After all, I was friendly with lots of boys and girls in our neighbourhood and at my school. Some were Jewish, others weren't. I knew that a few of the gentiles could be mean to the Jewish kids, but my friends weren't like that. What our different religions were didn't matter to us. We all just played together – football and drawing, building and marbles.

My best friend at school was Samuel Gold. He was Jewish too, and in the same grade as me. Sam was the class clown but super smart. He could read something once and remember it word for word. He had a photographic memory, he said. He was tall and skinny, with dark curly hair and the darkest skin I've ever seen. No freckles like Walter.

He was my other friend, Walter Kane. He had lots of freckles. He lived a few doors up from me. His father was Jewish but his mother wasn't. Sam and Walter and me – we used to play football together. Sam was best at drawing and marbles, and Walter was brilliant at soccer because he was small and very quick on his feet. I just loved kicking a ball, any ball. And most of our spare time together as friends was spent playing football – at school, in the yard or at the park on the weekends when it wasn't raining. Sometimes even when it was. We barracked for Pogon Lwów football team, Zayda's favourite team too. Zayda taught me the rules of football and all about the key players in the team. 'Sasha, always remember the three forwards!' Zayda would say enthusiastically. 'Kuchar, Batsch and Grabien. Brilliant players! Well over two hundred goals between them!'

One week we had a football match against another school and I had to play forward. Sam was centre forward because he was so tall. You could hear him screaming all the way back to Brody. 'Come on, Sasha! Wipe them out!' And I did. I loved the action, the excitement of the goal, the mud and the smell of the grass.

The girls at my school sometimes came to watch, but they usually played together. Sam and I would see them sometimes over in the meadows near home.

'You boys are just too boisterous for us,' one of the girls called Mina said. She liked using big words. 'Go and play somewhere else. You'll get mud on our dolls.' I quite liked Mina, though. She was tall and big for a girl, with sparkly blue eyes and her face would beam when she cuddled her doll and watched us play soccer. When it began to rain, Mina and her friends quickly packed up their dolls and headed for home.

'Which house are we feeding our dolls in today, Anka?' I heard her say. 'Yours or mine?'

'I think it's my turn. Come with me and we'll leave the boys to play. I've already set the table for *Shabbat*.' And the girls would run home, leaving Sam and me with the soccer ball. We didn't care about the mud or the rain and played until it began to get dark.

I suppose that's what Zayda meant about everyone getting on. All us children could do it. So I always thought the adults could too.

'But remember this, Sasha,' Zayda added that night, 'do not lose your faith. Faith is everything. You must remember this, no matter what.'

By now it was 1937. I was eight years old. And all around us in Poland people were getting angry with the Jews. Aunty Binka and Mama talked about it around the dinner table.

'But Larissa!' Binka almost cried, sounding afraid. 'We're not even allowed to go to university any more! At least not many of us! They won't let us be doctors or lawyers . . . They sack Jews from so many jobs!'

'I know it is bad, Binka. But it's much worse in Germany. Hitler's blaming the Jews for everything.'

'I'm frightened, Larissa. I'm frightened about how popular Hitler is. How can a man like that be so popular?'

I sat and listened and ate my bread and chicken soup and didn't really know or care who Hitler was. But I knew he made people nervous.

'Will I still be allowed to play football with Sam and Walter, in the park?'

'Sasha, for goodness sake, there are more important things to worry about than football!'

That was probably true, but I couldn't think of any just then. Sam and Walter and I were planning a match for the weekend.

Mama went on. 'He has promised the German people many things. Jobs and making Germany great again.'

'Yes, and he talks about the superiority of the Aryan race and our inferiority,' said Binka. 'He won't let us vote or marry gentiles. He won't let us use swimming pools or go to restaurants.' Binka was sounding more and more upset. 'He won't let us go to concerts or the theatre, Larissa! It might be Germany but it will only encourage people in Poland to hate us too.'

'Sshhhh, Binka! Think of Sasha!' Mama smiled at me, one of those fake smiles, and I just looked backwards and forwards from Mama to Binka and asked, 'Well, who is Hitler anyway? He will let me stay at my school, won't he? I like being with Sam and Walter.'

'Of course you do, Sasha.' She looked at Binka. 'We will all be fine, you'll see. Hitler is just a mad German.'

Binka tried to reassure me then. 'He's the ruler of Germany, Sasha. But don't you worry, your mama has a fine new job now,' she added, trying to change the subject.

'And I've made a new friend too,' Mama added. 'She's called Bella, and she is a very kind Polish gentile. And so very helpful to me. A lovely lady!'

I liked the sound of Bella and hoped that Mama would always have her as a friend. She made Mama happier, especially since she had missed her mother very much.

'Larissa, darling,' Binka said. 'Our lovely mama would want you to have friends like Bella. Oh, if only Mama hadn't died so young!'

They were talking about Bubbe. Mama's mother's real name was Freda Kohn, but we always called her Bubbe, as if I had a grandmother still, not just the memory of one. Binka told me of how Mama looked after Bubbe when she'd got sick. One day Bubbe started to cough. But the cough didn't go away. It got worse, and then after a few weeks, months maybe, she got really sick. So Mama hardly left her side, bringing her cold compresses for her head and warm broth. Mama had been a good nurse, a loving daughter and a good sister. But even so, Bubbe died in Mama's arms, of pneumonia, when Mama was only thirteen years old.

Even now when Mama talks about the day her mama died, tears roll down her face. 'But Sasha,' she said, 'she does not have to suffer any more. We have her memory to keep us warm, a picture of her to remind us, my darling.'

'Good heavens,' Binka said suddenly, changing the mood. 'What on earth would Bubbe think about Hitler if she knew what that dreadful man was up to?'

I didn't know it then. And I honestly wasn't too worried about mad Hitler. I had no idea how important Bella and good friends like that would become in our terrible days ahead.

Chapter 3
WAR STRIKES

1938. It wasn't long before the end of the year. It was cold. The frost had settled on the cobblestone streets, and the trees outside my bedroom were bare. I came home from school and saw Mama crying, leaning on the dining table and holding a letter in her hand. She was talking to Aunty Binka, and they didn't look like they'd want me to interrupt, so I hid behind the door to my bedroom before they could see me and listened to what they were saying.

'And then this letter came, this morning,' Mama said. 'It's from Aunt Matilde, Binka. Oh God. Listen...'

My dear Larissa,
My heart is heavy with sad news.
We have had a very bad time here in the last week. Your cousin Gisa is writing a journal, recording what life in Germany is like for us now. We want you to know what is happening here so I've enclosed a copy of her

entry from 10 November. This is what she's written:

'Last night, heavy clouds of smoke billowed from the burning synagogues, torched by members of the Nazi SA. Storm troopers, "Brownshirts", they call them. Hitler's private army. We could hear screams from houses as Jewish homes were vandalised. Paintings were slashed, eiderdowns ripped to shreds, chairs smashed apart. The sound of crunching glass echoed in the darkness of this cold wet night. The streets were littered with glittering glass.'

Mama paused. I could hear her sob.

'There was so much noise and screaming. I could hear footsteps and banging downstairs. Storm troopers were inside our house, tearing and smashing everything they could. They locked Mama and Papa in the bathroom. I could hear them shouting. The men, reeking of alcohol, stormed into my room and tore away the eiderdown that

> *covered me in my bed. They pulled me out of bed, ripping my nightgown, and ordered me to get dressed. I was terrified. But they were laughing, and then they overturned my dressing table and wardrobe and left.*
>
> *'I was lucky. We heard later that the Nazis murdered many Jews last night, and thousands of others were sent to labour camps.'*

Mama stopped reading. 'That is the end of that entry. Oh Binka! This is ... inhuman! They are calling it *Kristallnacht*, the night of the broken glass. The Nazis smashed all the shop windows and homes and hospitals too, and schools! Writing horrible things about us on the walls! Even Jewish cemeteries. Looting and killing ...'

I peered round the door frame and saw Mama staring at Binka with a terrified look on her face. Aunty Binka was silent. Then after a while she said, 'I've heard about such things in the newspapers. How can this be? Germany is such a cultured country.' Binka's voice was calmer than Mama's.

'It's not going to stop, is it, Binka?'

'I'd like to reassure you, Larissa. But I fear the violence might spread even to Poland.'

I think I made a slight noise then, and Mama and Binka stopped talking. I ducked further behind the door and snuck quickly back to my bedroom.

Later I heard Binka leave – she must have gone to the shops or something – and she said to Mama near the door, 'Poor little Sasha! The child does not yet understand the horrors of the world in which we live.'

By the time the New Year came – it was 1939 and I'd turned ten already – life in Poland had become much more difficult. For one thing, Mama started to complain about the price of food.

'Why is everything so expensive?' she said to Binka.

'Well, there'll be tough times ahead, Larissa, you know this, and we have to make the best of it. We'll stock up on things we can store – tinned sardines, beans and a little salted meat, condensed milk, Sasha likes that – and cereals and flour will keep. Sugar and salt. We just have to be clever.' She smiled at Mama.

Mama and I went out to buy lots of coal for the following winter too. 'We must keep warm, after all, Sasha.'

Mama and Binka, and Aunty Rena too, all followed the news about Nazi Germany every day. I knew they were scared. There'd been rumours, Mama said, about money being frozen in the banks, so she exchanged some Polish *zlotys* for American dollars. It was enough for us to get by, but not much more. I remember thinking that it was a very strange thing to do, to freeze money. It's not like it goes off, like fish or anything. But I was only ten.

And the adults were scared about what Hitler was doing to other countries too. He'd already decided Austria was his, and most of Czechoslovakia as well. Hitler wanted to make Germany bigger, by taking other people's land, so the Germans could have more living space – *Lebensraum*, he called it. I wondered why we couldn't have more living space too, here in Poland. Some days I'd ask Sam about things like this.

'Sam, do your parents talk about Hitler much?'

'Yeah, all the time. It's boring.'

'Are you scared of him?'

'Me? Course not. You?'

'No, course not.' But I'm pretty sure I didn't sound convincing.

We were playing with some old marbles I'd found in a drawer in our living room that day. Sam was quiet, and I liked spending time with him because he enjoyed the same games I liked. He'd invent completely new games too, and never talked too much and always had brilliant ideas for new rules and ways of doing things.

Sam looked at me a bit closer. 'Don't worry, Sash. Hitler's only interested in Germany really. He'll leave us alone. You'll see.' And he went back to sorting some glass marbles into different sizes and colours. Sam seemed so unconcerned about the world out there. Anything beyond our street corner didn't seem to worry him, as long as he had enough time to kick a ball around.

'Come on, Sam. Let's take the soccer ball and go to the meadow for a bit.' I was getting tired of marbles.

Sam and I ran down the stairs and out the front doors of our apartment building and across the laneway next door, following the street past the park and out towards the meadow. We liked this particular meadow because it was quiet and away from the noise of the main town. We could play there for as long as we wanted on most days.

We'd got to the edge of the meadow when Sam suddenly grabbed me and pulled me back by the shoulder.

'Hey! What did you do that for?' I said. 'We're just about there.'

'Shh! Look!' Sam said. He pointed to the far side of the meadow where we usually played soccer while the girls set their dolls up under the trees.

'What?'

And then I saw what he meant.

Soldiers.

Brownshirts.

'Get back, Sasha,' said Sam. 'Come on, let's get out of here!'

'But what about the ball?'

'I'm not playing with them around!'

'But . . . look . . . what're they doing?'

We watched for a moment, hidden by the trees. There were four German soldiers and they seemed to be talking to each other and looking into the trees as though there was something very interesting in there. Then suddenly one of the soldiers grabbed at a large object – something in the bushes, like a large sack or something – pulled it out and threw it onto the ground in front of him. He shot at it, kicked it, and the four soldiers moved on.

'What is it, Sam? I can't see! What did they just do?'

But Sam had gone very quiet. He wasn't usually quiet. 'Come on, Sash. Let's get out of here.'

'But why? What was that thing?'

Sam didn't say much. He just grabbed my shoulder again and started to walk quietly back towards the street. He looked pale and very frightened.

'Sam?'

'Nothin'.'

'What did the soldiers shoot?'

'What d'you *think* they shot?' he said almost angrily. 'A Jew of course.'

We soon found out that shootings were becoming common around our town. And that Hitler wanted more than just Germany. Newspapers began to report that he'd demanded the return of parts of Poland, and that Britain had promised to help us if we were invaded. Mama and Binka talked about nothing else.

'But surely it won't come to that?' Binka was starting to sound as afraid as Mama.

But it did. On 1 September that year, 1939, and just before Sam's birthday, our worst fears came true. Hitler invaded Poland from the east. Within days, Britain and France had declared war on Germany.

Mama and Binka tried very hard to talk about it without me in the room. But I knew. I listened and lay awake at night and followed their conversations. I talked to my friends, well, Sam anyway, and listened to his parents. We wanted to know. Knowing was better than not knowing. At least that's what I thought.

'There was heavy bombing last night, Binka. Cities and villages, all just smoky grey rubble. Everything is destroyed – railway stations, bridges, beautiful buildings. Homes burnt to cinders, roofs blown away, and the people!'

'No one expected this, Larissa, not such calamity in Poland. But let's not alarm Sasha. We must reassure him.'

Later that week, I can't remember exactly what day, but it was still early September, I came home from school and was a bit later than usual because I'd been playing with Sam and Walter behind the railway station. We'd been messing about building miniature roads and buildings in the gravel by the side of an abandoned railway track. We'd been there for at least an hour. But then Walter said he had to go because he'd cut his finger on a sharp stone. Didn't look too bad to me, but we took him home anyway, and just as I got in our front door, I heard explosions. I couldn't tell where the noise came from but it sounded like it came from the direction of the railway where we'd just been playing.

I stayed in my room for the rest of the day, reading and listening to the noises outside, until Mama came home, rushing in the door. The first thing she did was run to my room and hug me hard. She'd been crying and her clothes were all messy. 'Oh Sasha! Oh Sasha!' she kept saying. 'You are safe!'

This was the first of many days of bombing in Lwów, but everyone, us included, just tried to carry on as usual. Cinemas and cafes stayed open, except all the lifts were stopped for some reason, and Binka said the universities even continued teaching. Maybe they could teach countries how to stop arguing with each other and dropping bombs, I thought.

For now, I was still allowed to go to school. Sam, Walter and Mina went too. Mama kept telling us not to be alarmed. 'Yes, Sasha, it is true there is some political unrest in Poland at the moment, but don't be too worried. Even Binka says it will pass soon.'

But I knew that wasn't true. Mama and Binka were frightened and uncertain of what lay ahead for us. Sam and I had heard stories about Jewish people being shot on the spot by Germans in Warsaw and Krakow, and Mama worried that if ever the Germans got here . . .

It turned out she was right. On 12 September, the Germans reached Lwów.

'It's a siege, Sasha. The Germans have surrounded us. But the Polish Army will defend us, you'll see.'

Except the bombs didn't stop. Soon after that, our Lwów radio station in Batory Street was demolished by the *Luftwaffe*. That's what they called the German air force. I thought it was a funny-sounding name, one of those words you try to say, really fast, over and over without messing it up. Sam was better at it than me. He'd go on and on. '*Luftwaffeluftwaffeluftwaffe.*' And of course he'd always win.

Then the soldiers from the Soviet Union came . . .

That day I snuck outside and hid in a laneway next to our apartment. I wanted to see what the Red Army and the Soviets actually looked like. And I was so surprised, because they looked ragged and messy in their khaki uniforms – their trousers and jackets and dark boots were old and dirty, and their hats looked ragged. It wasn't how I'd imagined a powerful army at all. There were others who wore helmets with a red star in the middle – maybe they were officers, I wasn't sure. One thing I was sure of, though – they stank. All of them. A stench of dirt and sweat passed over me as they marched by. Some stopped and began to talk to people on the streets. They spoke Russian and I couldn't understand much, but then others began to speak Polish and told the people who'd gathered on the streets about justice and liberation for Poland.

Eventually I snuck back inside. I felt confused. I didn't understand why the Soviet Union wanted to invade too, especially with such a dirty army.

'Everybody wants land, Sasha,' said Mama. 'The Soviets want eastern Poland and Lwów. Germany will take western Poland. The country will be divided. But maybe . . . maybe we will be better off with the Russians. At least they are promising equality.'

'I'm not so sure, Larissa,' Binka scoffed. 'Many Jews will leave.'

'Many are coming *here*!' Mama said. 'They are flooding into Lwów, away from the Germans at least, hoping for a safer life here.'

'And others have gone.'

'Yes, I know. Tylda has gone already, Binka. To America she said, her whole family. Gisa and her parents – gone too. Anyone who can afford it is leaving. To Mexico, Argentina, Brazil – even Shanghai. Anywhere but here!' Mama was becoming more and more upset.

'It will be all right, Larissa. You'll see.' Binka took Mama's hand in hers and gave it a good squeeze.

Mama sighed. 'I wish I had enough money to take Sasha and all of us to America too.'

Suddenly I brightened. America! I wondered what living in America would be like. As I lay in bed at night, kept awake by the noise of the bombings and explosions, America seemed like a wonderful dream. I thought of Tylda and wondered if she'd made it safely to America. Maybe she'd meet famous people, actors like Cary Grant. She used to go on and on about how handsome he was. Whenever she found a photograph of him in a magazine or a picture-show annual, she'd just drool over him. I'd roll my eyes at her. But now, the thought of Cary Grant and film stars and being in America suddenly seemed very appealing – to be away from the noise of the bombs. They never seemed to stop.

'When will the noise end, Mama? Why's this happening anyway?'

'The city feels like an earthquake has hit it,' Mama said. 'The ground is shaking,'

I snuggled up against Mama that night, and we both watched the flickers of flame pulsing in the darkness outside. 'Tell me a story, Mama. I don't want to listen to the noise outside.'

Mama laughed. 'You are like Bubbe, Sasha. She was always such a great storyteller. When I was your age I would snuggle up with her in front of a crackling fire and she would tell me stories all about Brody and Schwabendorf. D'you know what she used to say to me, Sasha?'

'What?' I heard another bomb in the distance.

'She used to say, "Larissa darling, love does strange things to people. Love makes us do extraordinary things."'

'It does?'

'You will learn of this one day, Sasha. Now, what story would you like?'

'The one about Hershl!'

'Hershl the tailor?'

'Yes! That one.'

So Mama began, 'Once upon a time, there was a tailor in Brody called Hershl. He was a bull-necked man, with big shoulders and bushy black eyebrows... and his wife was very round and jolly.'

I laughed and was glad my mind was taken away from the bombs at last.

'Hershl's most favourite things to eat in the whole world were *golabki* – cabbage rolls, and baked duck too. But even more that this, he most loved to eat the *makowiec* his wife would make for him – the delicious poppyseed cake.'

'So do I! Moist and scrumptious.' I said, licking my lips hoping that Mama would make some *makowiec* soon too.

Mama went on with her story that evening, telling me all about the greed of the tailor and how fat he grew and how he eventually ran off with Zelda who was half his age, and how his poor wife thought that her delicious food would keep her husband tied to her for all time.

'But food isn't everything, Sasha. We need love too.'

I understood what Mama meant, but I just liked the way she told the story and of how funny she made the tailor sound. By the end I'd forgotten all about the bombs.

Sometimes I was sad that I couldn't hear Bubbe's

version of that story. It would've been something! Mama always told me over and over how good a storyteller Bubbe had been.

It was almost the end of September by now – a sunny autumn day. I was kicking my old football around in the laneway by myself, feeling bored because Sam and Walter weren't allowed out that day, when I heard the beginnings of a strange sound. I didn't recognise it straight away, coming from a distance – sharp and hollow. I ran onto the main street to see what it was. Many people gathered around to see. The noise was coming closer and getting louder. I'd never heard a sound like it before. But then I recognised it – horses! It was the sharp, clinking sound of horses' hooves on the cobblestones of Lwów.

Then from around the corner and into the main square there came some beautiful white horses, ridden by Soviet soldiers, headed down the main city street. The soldiers on these horses looked clean and fresh, in smart uniforms, much nicer than the others I'd seen. These ones looked proud, parading and celebrating their victory over the Germans and the capture of Lwów from Nazi hands.

Three soldiers lead the way – the middle one bearing the Soviet flag. More soldiers lined the streets on foot. I wondered who'd be right – Mama or

Binka – and whether our life under Soviet rule would be better or worse.

It was around this time that Mama's hometown of Brody was occupied by the Soviets too. Zayda still lived there and we were all concerned about his safety under Soviet rule. So in the New Year of 1940, Mama wrote to him about the changes in Lwów, hoping for some news. It'd been ages since we'd heard from Zayda.

'What did you say to Zayda, Mama? In the letter? Did you ask him if he was playing chess still?'

'Of course, Sasha. I asked him how they all are. Life must have changed for them too. For all of them.'

'Did you tell him I was home from school now?'

'Yes, Sasha. I told him you are well and eating us out of house and home! Now go and find something to do. I am busy.'

But I knew Mama didn't want me to know what else she'd written. I knew she'd told him our lives weren't easy now. When we went to buy food there was nothing left on the shelves. We had to queue for bread. Last week Binka had to wait fifteen hours for meat. Coal was hard to get too, and I was glad Mama stocked up on it before things got so bad.

'Ordinary folk are suffering more and more, the wealthy too.' I heard Mama and Binka talking again. 'Businessmen have no money. Jews and gentiles alike are arrested and deported to the Soviet Union. There is only fear and mistrust.'

I knew what the Soviets looked like now, in the streets with their red armbands. Mama said a member of the Communist Party was now her boss at work. 'He knows *nothing*,' Mama said in disgust. 'Every five minutes he calls me in to ask me endless stupid questions!'

But she was much happier when a letter of reply finally arrived from Zayda. She wouldn't let me read it, but I snuck out from my room one day and found it in a kitchen drawer.

```
July 1940
Dear Larissa,
   Life is hard here. We are all well,
but not so good in spirit.
   I am still managing the timber mill.
As in Lwów, there are changes in
Brody under the Soviets. Factories and
stores have been nationalised. Jewish
owners can only work there as managers
or skilled craftsmen. Important
merchants, manufacturers and community
leaders have been exiled to Russia.
   I must return to work now. I am
constantly watched. I am lucky they
```

*did not send me to Russia. Larissa,
I am sorry to say they took most of
our land.*

Call or write when you can.

Look after yourself, my child.

*Your loving father,
Richard*

I was disappointed Zayda hadn't mentioned me or the chess games. Maybe it was because his land had been taken away and he had to work so much. Just like Mama now – not enough time to be happy. His letter seemed very short. He used to write lots of things and have lots of time.

Mama was busy now too because she'd started learning Russian. Mama was always very good at schoolwork when she was little and used to teach other students sometimes. She was good at languages and bought lots of books. So she'd be good at learning Russian, I thought. I wondered if Zayda had to learn Russian. Mama had a head start but, even so, when she started to find the Russian hard to learn she turned to her friend Bella for help.

Bella Kowalski was a very smart lady, like Mama. She'd replaced her husband at the oil company where they used to work together, and she was fluent in Russian. She had gone to the University of Leningrad before the war and now helped Mama learn Russian some evenings after work.

'I do not like these staff meetings, Bella. All this new Russian stuff at work. The Soviets want to brainwash us into loving Joseph Stalin! It's disgusting!'

'Yes but Larissa dear, we must at least pretend to listen. You don't want to end up being transported to Siberia.'

This frightened me so much, the thought of being sent to a place like Siberia where it was icy and freezing. It was cold enough here in Lwów. But the far north-eastern corner of Russia?

'You spoke well at the meeting the other day, Bella. You were brave, speaking in Polish.'

'Polish is my mother tongue! They cannot force me to speak in Russian. It's time the Soviets learnt to speak Polish anyway. They live in a Polish country, by choice. They keep saying to us that our lives are so good. I would like to ask them: if our lives are meant to be so good now, why are they so bad? We're deprived of everything and you Soviets have all the privileges! Where is your sense of justice? We work hard, earn low salaries, and we do not get equal treatment!'

A cold shiver ran down my spine. I'd never heard Bella sound so angry.

'Bella, please! Do not get into trouble. The Soviets don't show what they really think. Don't pay for your courage and outspokenness. They will investigate you, you know that.' Mama paused. 'Perhaps it's best if you don't come into the office tomorrow. Go and hide. You took a huge risk opening your mouth. The Soviets could deport you.'

'Oh don't be silly, Larissa. I have to go in tomorrow. I am needed badly to translate that government initiative. And you need me to translate other documents. I'll take a few days leave after that. I promise.'

I went to bed that night feeling very scared for Bella. I didn't like most of the conversations I heard the adults have these days. They all sounded scared. And adults weren't meant to be scared. Something bad was about to happen. I knew it. And, sooner than I thought, I was proven right.

Chapter 4

BELLA KOWALSKI

When Bella discovered the news, she was with us in our apartment.

She didn't scream or cry or anything. Her voice was calm and quiet. She was so brave. I didn't think I would be as brave as that. She reminded me of Sam the day we'd seen the soldiers in the meadow.

'My husband,' she said to Mama. 'Did you know Boris had been taken as a prisoner of war, to a camp? Well, I knew that. But I wondered how he was.'

'Oh Bella...' Mama knew she was about to hear bad news.

'And so now...' Bella seemed to gather strength. 'And now, they have... executed him.'

She stopped. 'And he was so gentle and so kind.' She looked at Mama. 'I think I will want to fight even harder now, you know. We must fight, Larissa. Fight this oppression, stand up to these dictators.'

Many Polish officers like Bella's husband, Boris, had been transported to the Soviet Union. I knew because I'd heard my friends talking about the prisoner-of-war camps. I heard people had to work at hard labour, or they were shot. I heard about what had happened last April: the Soviets had executed thousands of officers in the Katyn Forest outside Smolensk near Moscow. They killed police and members of the Polish intelligentsia. We heard that mass executions had become common, but this one in April had been the largest so far.

Bella continued to come around to our place after that, and taught Mama Russian. Sometimes we'd go to Bella's house too, for supper or lunch together. One day we were running late for lunch and Mama hurried me into my coat.

'Sasha, come on now! We are off to Bella's this afternoon, remember? We will have tea, and you can read your book while Bella and I get some work done.'

'I am reading *Anna Karenina*,' I said proudly.

'Don't be silly, Sasha. It's far too big a book for you. Go and find something more your age. Hurry now!'

So I ran quickly into my room and picked one of my smaller books about magicians. I replaced the Tolstoy next to Mama's collection of stories in the hall. I planned to try and read it soon anyway. I'd heard a lot about *Anna Karenina*. It had trains in it, and a very gruesome scene at the end.

So we rugged up against the cold, and I tucked the

smaller book into the inside pocket of my coat and left with Mama to go to visit Bella.

We walked the short distance to Bella's place through the cobblestones of the market square and past the rows and rows of different-coloured apartment buildings. We reached the front door of Bella's apartment, and Mama was about to knock on the door when she noticed something wasn't right.

'That's odd,' she said quietly. 'The door is not locked.'

It was true. I could see the door was slightly open. It made me nervous. I was always nervous going to Bella's anyway because the smell of the stairs and the damp of the corridor and the grime on the banisters reminded me of ghost stories I'd read.

'Mama...'

'Stay here in the corridor until I come back. I won't be long.' She pushed the door of Bella's apartment open and went quietly into the entrance hall.

I was too afraid to move anyway, so I just stood there and listened as hard as I could. I heard Mama gasp, then a noise like a chair scraping and people struggling. Someone shouted in Russian.

And then Mama said something, but in English, and a man's voice yelled back. 'You bloody bitch! I'll shoot you! Both of you! Enough *Polish* and your causes!'

There was more scuffling and I think Bella made some sort of noise. Then Mama was talking again, in a different way this time, calm and soothing. It was very strange, but I was so scared I just stood in the corridor, frozen to the spot, waiting to hear what would happen next.

'But Comrade,' I heard Mama say calmly. 'It's a wonderful evening out there tonight! Let's go for a walk together. Why don't you get dressed and come with me?'

There was a pause. I couldn't hear what was happening. Then the man said, 'But why would *you* go with me?'

'Comrade, surely I don't have to spell it out! A wonderful night together! Some wine! You've been stuck in this place too long. Let's have a good time. Come on!'

The man again... sounding gruff and scary. 'I will get dressed. Wait for me.' I heard a door shut somewhere inside.

Then suddenly Mama and Bella came running out. They grabbed me so fast I didn't have time to think or say anything or react at all, but I ran as fast as I could as Mama hauled me into the street below, all of us frightened and shaking and running for our lives.

'Oh I cannot go back there, Larissa!' Bella cried as

we ran further and further towards the main square. 'I can never go back. To my *own* apartment!'

By the time we got home my legs were aching and I had no breath left to speak. The man from Bella's apartment hadn't followed us, but even so Mama locked our door and drew the curtains. She prepared a hot bath for Bella and made up a spare bed on the sofa in the living room. I was sent to bed early. Not once did they talk to me about what had happened or tell me who that man was or why Bella had bruises on her face. But I knew they were staying up and talking about him that evening; he was Russian, a soldier, he had made her terribly afraid, I think he threatened to kill her, and the soldier had been drunk, Bella said. They talked about it the whole evening. Eventually I couldn't stay awake any longer, trying to work out what Bella would do and what they were saying. But I knew she would have to find somewhere else to live.

By next morning when I woke, Mama was sitting in the kitchen, and Bella was gone.

'I have to go to work now, Sasha. Stay indoors. Don't answer the door. Binka will look after you. I will be back as soon as I can.'

'But where is Bella?'

'At work, Sasha. She is fine. Now go and read. I must go.'

So Mama went to work, and I wondered if Bella really would be there. Maybe she'd been arrested. So many people were arrested these days. She was anti-communist and the wife of a Polish major. That was more than enough to get her arrested.

Mama said nothing more about the Bella incident that week. Then a letter arrived. It was from Bella. She was safe, it said, but she needed Mama to go to her apartment and get some things for her. She'd send someone to collect them from our apartment.

I knew Mama was scared. She had me to consider, and Binka and Rena. What was she to do? She had to help Bella, but what about that drunken soldier? He might still be there. He might kill her. But Bella's housemaid, Irena, was still living in her apartment too. They'd been together for twenty years, and Bella treated her with kindness and generosity. Bella had earned her maid's loyalty. And because the communists wouldn't let people employ maids, Irena had pretended to be a relative while she secretly worked as Bella's maid instead.

So Mama wrote a note to Irena, explaining the situation, and asked her to pack a bag of the things Bella had requested, and deliver it by messenger. Irena sent a message back – and did as suggested. Mama never had to go back to the apartment herself at all. I was glad about that!

But while Mama and Irena were making these plans, bigger things were happening all around us. I heard about them from friends, from Binka and Rena, from anywhere I could get an idea of what was going on. It was June 1941 by now. Germany invaded the Soviet Union.

And then in July, the pogrom came to Lwów. I will never forget it. Thousands of Jews were dragged from their homes, beaten to death or simply shot on the spot. I couldn't stop myself – I watched this happening from my bedroom window. Even Mama didn't stop me after a while. She knew there was no hiding from the truth now, not even for me. So through my bedroom window I watched – watched an old Jewish man forced by the Nazis onto his knees and made to clean the gutter with a toothbrush. Others were forced to pick up horse manure and put it in their hats. It wasn't the physical torture of it I hated, even though that was hard to watch. It was the humiliation, the onlookers who laughed and watched and did nothing. I couldn't understand why. The Jews had become a show. I felt sick, seeing so much cruelty, and I became terribly afraid about what might happen to us.

That week was the beginning of the end of life in Lwów. That was the end of anything that might have felt like a normal life. Soon the Germans started to bomb again. The Red Army suffered heavy losses and abandoned our city. On one sunny summer's day, Hitler's *Panzers* invaded. We were defenceless. Our city was on the brink of destruction. Terror hit. A hundred thousand Jews – people just like me and Mama and Bella – were at the mercy of the Nazis.

I continued to watch all this from my bedroom window, pulled the curtains open and saw the commotion in the streets, people swarming everywhere as the Germans entered our beautiful city. There were boys and girls about my age down there in the streets too, and they seemed to watch in awe, clapping and welcoming the soldiers into Lwów. I couldn't take my eyes off all the steel helmets, the rifles and the mass of grey-green jackets. Soldiers looked out from trucks, transporting people through the streets, and they too were watching. But it was the wrong way around. They were observing us, and we were the animals in a zoo.

How could people believe that life under the Germans would be better? It didn't look better. Nothing was safe any more. And very soon after that day we were proven right – we heard of thousands of Jews being dragged from their homes, beaten and executed. Now it wasn't just one or two German soldiers around, or isolated incidents like that day in the meadow. Now it was everywhere.

Mama and Binka spoke about Jewish women who were shoved and kicked and beaten in the face, not just with hands but with sticks and rifles and tools. I couldn't undertand how no one helped them. Didn't anybody have a heart? Some were pulled by the hair and thrown around. Once Binka and I watched a woman stripped naked until she had only one long sock and a shoe left on, and she was pushed to the ground while others around her ran naked and screaming through the street. I thought it couldn't get worse – there could be nothing next. But there was always more.

In the first few days, the Nazis recruited a Ukrainian police force and Jews for assistance to clean out the prisons in Lwów. We heard that Jews were beaten there, even thrown out of windows from the higher floors. Mama gave up trying to hide anything at all from me now. The truth was inescapable. I saw it all around me, outside in the streets, in the faces of my aunts. We were told by survivors that many others were machine-gunned or hit by grenades. Victims were forced to watch others being murdered before they were killed themselves. Later, we heard that more than three thousand Jews did not get out of the prisons alive.

Of course I didn't go to school. I hadn't been for months. I wasn't even sure if my school was there any more. I missed my friends. I wondered what was happening to them too. By now I'd lost touch with Sam and Walter and I had no way of checking or knowing anything about them. We stayed locked in our apartment, with the food we had stored and nothing to do but watch and listen.

Mama came in to sit on my bed and hold me tight as we listened to the disturbances outside in the street. 'Mama, I heard what you said about the Jews in Lwów prison.' I stopped and looked at Mama's face. Her eyes were red and swollen, as if she'd been crying all day. 'If the Germans capture us, we'd end up like them, wouldn't we? I listen to you and Binka talking sometimes...'

'Oh Sasha!' Mama said, and she squeezed my hand like she always did when she was trying to be reassuring. But she didn't know what to say now. Even though she thought the same as me, she didn't want to frighten me. It didn't matter. I was already frightened.

I sat there on my bed and looked at her face. 'Mama, how are we going to keep safe?'

She still didn't know what to say. She squeezed my hand again. 'Sasha darling, you are asking all the right questions. And I will try to explain a little bit to you. The streets of our city are no longer safe for the Jewish people.'

I knew that already. I'd known that from the time

in the meadow with Sam. I'd never told Mama about the shooting we'd seen that day.

'And now the Nazis have said that we must all wear armbands. They are white, with a blue Star of David on them, so people can tell that we are Jews.'

'But why? Why are Jews so special all of a sudden?'

Mama had no answer to my questions now. At least I had my books to read. Sam must surely be doing the same, I thought. He'd be with his mother and father and little sister. I missed hanging out with Sam and Walter and playing football with them. I wondered whether Walter was safer than most because his mother wasn't Jewish. Sometimes I'd think about them and get my old football out when Mama and Binka were asleep and kick it gently around my room so I wouldn't wake them up. It was better than nothing.

That week, from my bedroom window, I saw Jews once more being beaten by the Germans. They used what looked like iron canes, heavy and deadly. I saw them strip women again and beat them, and I couldn't believe how the skin just seemed to rip away from their bodies and the women would be shaking and crying, and no one would stop. I thought of Mama and Binka and Aunty Rena, and I turned away and curled up under the blankets on my bed.

Some days the Germans seemed to swarm all over our streets. I saw Ukrainian police too. They were on the

Germans' side, and they kicked Jews for not cleaning up the streets properly. There was charred wood, and burned iron and nails and all sorts of junk all over the streets now, from the bombs and the German air raids.

'We are being hunted like animals!' Binka cried. 'I'm too afraid even to look out the door!'

One evening our neighbour from the downstairs apartment, Mrs Brott, came to talk to Mama.

'I have news. More news. Terrible news! Have you heard?'

'About what, Sima?' Mama, Rena and Binka looked at each other. They didn't even bother telling me to go to my room now.

'About the *Einsatzgruppen*.'

'The what?'

'They are prowling the streets of Lwów, rounding people up. Anyone that they think is a political enemy. Gypsies, and Jews. Just three days ago, they transported a whole crowd of Jews into the woods outside town. The rumours are that they disappeared.'

'The *Einsatzgruppen*...'

'They are meant to be *educated* men! How can educated men do this?'

'They're fanatics, Larissa. Nazis. They will do anything.'

I thought of what Mama used to say about my papa, how he was an educated man, gentle, who used his education to help others. How could men who were clever and educated be murderers?

Mama and my aunts, all of us, were in so much danger now.

'Well then,' said Mama. 'There is nothing for it. We must prepare to leave.'

Shortly after Mrs Brott went back to her apartment, there was another knock on our door. Mama didn't want to answer that one, but the banging became fierce and she had no choice.

'Quickly, Sasha!' she whispered. 'We are going to pretend we're sick in bed. Here...' She and Binka grabbed hand towels from the bathroom, wet them under the tap and held them to their foreheads. 'We'll put wet towels on our faces. Like this.'

'But how long will I have to do that for?' I asked. I thought this was stupid. I was nearly twelve, but Mama never seemed to have answers for my questions now. She'd always had the answers when I was little. Now I was just tired of doing things I didn't understand. I remembered what Zayda had said about thinking for myself. But I didn't know what to think. Every day brought more bad news. Things seemed to get worse and worse.

But as an even louder series of knocks banged against our door, Mama took control. 'Sasha, for *God's* sake be quiet now! Let me do the talking!'

Mama smoothed her hands over her clothes, and quietly stepped to the door and opened it. She was in her dressing gown and slippers, and she pressed the wet towel to her forehead, moaning. I thought it was quite a good act.

A group of angry-looking Ukrainians with large sticks barged in, I am not sure how many, and Mama returned to me and pushed me back into my bedroom. 'Go back to bed, Sasha. You are too ill to get up yet.' So I did as I was told and lay down on my bed, and Binka lay very still beside me. The Ukrainians began to search our apartment, looking for Jews.

I heard Mama try to reason with the soldiers as she followed them around our home in their hunt.

'Look, we are ill. Please leave us alone. We have nothing,' Mama said in a broken voice. The men gave her only a grunt in reply, and then they just seemed to leave. Mama came in to me and hugged me and Binka tight. Her dressing gown was wet with perspiration. I started to shake, and she hugged me even tighter, not knowing why the soldiers had spared us. 'It's all right, Sasha!' Mama said over and over. 'It's all right. We are all right!'

It was one of the many times I would have to pretend to be something that I wasn't.

Chapter 5
FLIGHT

The next day, Mrs Wolanski came to see Mama. She was the old Jewish woman who lived in the apartment next to ours. I was a little bit scared of her because she'd always look at me as though I'd already done something wrong. She wheezed when she spoke, and had thick black hair tied back in a tight bun. She could make me feel guilty just with one stare on some days. But she was kind and sometimes she'd bake a *kugel* and bring it around for us – noodles mixed with butter, eggs and cheese baked in a hot oven. I got hungry just thinking about it!

But today she didn't come around with *kugel*. She came quickly into our apartment, shutting the door quietly behind her. Mrs Wolanski looked agitated about something, and that made me even more scared of her than usual.

'Larissa, I tried to get food within the set times the Nazis have ordered, but there's nothing left. Nothing! Before long, we will all starve under these barbarians!'

'Yes, I know, Paula. Believe me, I know!'

'Do you know how unsafe it is in the streets now? Organised patrols hunt for Jews. Hitler's mobile killing units!' She lowered her voice. '*Thousands* have been taken to the power station in Pelczynska Street. Remember the construction worker, Schmuel Levine? He and his friends were forced to work for the Nazis. Others have been trucked to the woods, and we know they've been killed. And I haven't seen the Levy family for weeks! I heard that some of them even had to dig their own graves! Oh God, what is next for us?' I could see her eyes were full of tears.

'It is all right, Paula. It is bad, but we will be all right.' I think Mama was saying this just because she knew I'd be listening.

'But I heard too, from Sima, that the Nazis force Jews to clean toilets or make them crawl on their hands and knees and bark like dogs. And then some get hard labour . . .'

All of this was true. I'd seen the trucks outside. I'd seen what they made people do.

By now, the Nazis had set up the *Judenrat* in Lwów. It was a sort of council, Mama said, headed by a man called Dr Parnas.

'He is a Jewish lawyer, Sasha. Councils like this, well, they've been around for a while now in Poland. But the *Judenrat* . . .'

'What about the *Judenrat*?' I asked. Not that I really wanted to know any more. It all sounded pretty horrible.

'Well, there are twelve, maybe more, twenty-four members even, who are nominated by our fellow Jews. You know, rabbis or other learned citizens.'

'Why?'

'Sasha! Always "why" with you!'

'Zayda says I should question things, Mama. So I'm questioning.'

'All right, Sasha. Well, these men are wealthy and learned. They have influence – and authority. So they are invited to become members. The Nazis have to approve their membership.'

'What do they do when they get to be members?' It sounded like a school club to me.

'The *Judenrat* have to carry out Nazi orders. Things about the Jewish community, our food and shelter, and sanitation. I don't know – our general welfare, I suppose. The daily life of our Jewish community.'

'We can do that ourselves, can't we?'

'The Nazis don't seem to think so.'

'Will you join the *Judenrat*, Mama?'

'Heavens no, Sasha! I won't be asked to join, not me!'

But Mama was wrong. That week she *was* asked to join.

She refused.

I think she refused because deep down she knew the Nazis would never look after our needs. She knew the *Judenrat* was about controlling the Jews, not looking after them.

But by refusing to help she was putting us in a lot of danger.

Mama turned out to be right, though. She somehow found out, maybe from some of our neighbours who'd already joined, that members of the *Judenrat* had to obey Nazi orders – to the letter. Jews like Mama tried to negotiate, to bargain so that we'd get a better deal. But from what Mama said they didn't always agree with the Nazis, or at least the Nazis didn't always agree with us, and when this happened arrests were made. That's why I was so afraid of Mama joining.

I'd heard things too – things that Binka said. Things that Mrs Wolanski said. People like Mama who didn't do what the Nazis wanted were taken to labour camps. I knew what that meant. It meant they were murdered.

Later, much later, I heard that even Yosef Parnas was shot. He'd refused to nominate thousands of Jews for deportation.

And then there were the ghettos.

I'd heard about places where Jews were made to

stay, all in one place, surrounded by barbed wire, brick walls and armed guards. They even had to build the brick walls themselves.

By November we heard that a ghetto like this had been made in one of the poorest areas of Lwów. It wasn't all that far from where we lived either. It was looked after by the *Judenrat*, and Jews were ordered to move there by the Nazis. Mama felt very scared about going into the ghetto. So did I. I liked my bedroom and I liked being close to my friends even though I couldn't see them any more and didn't know if they were even alive. Still, I was home. And home was home.

Mama refused to go to the ghetto. She wouldn't even listen to Binka about it. 'For God's sake, Binka, can't you hear yourself? In the ghetto we will all be destroyed! Destroyed! Like rats! I know it. We will *never* survive! Once we get inside we are dead.'

'Well, what will we do then?' Binka sounded annoyed. 'Tell me that, Larissa! Tell me! What will we do?'

Mama was silent. I knew that meant she was thinking carefully, working out what to say to Aunty Binka that would make her listen. So then Mama said, calmly and quietly, 'We will take Sasha and go to Brody. That's what we will do. I will try to let Father know. And I will figure out what to do from there.'

I liked that idea. I would be with Zayda again and we would play chess. Mama was such a smart person.

'Larissa, but all Jews have to go into the ghetto. There are orders!'

'We will *not* do what we are supposed to do then!' She sounded like she was spitting at someone the way she said that. 'We will *not* wear the Star of David on our arm. We will *not* register for the ghetto. If we do that it will be our *end*, Binka! Think! Think of who you are. That's how we survive, Binka. By remembering who we are!'

Mama calmed herself a bit, and spoke more slowly. 'I have to work out a plan. I need to think. Let's go home to Brody first.'

I was proud of my mama that day. Mama's decision saved us. The Lwów ghetto was unsanitary and overcrowded. We'd heard this. But here at home, even with all the shortages and dangers, she still managed to get eggs and potatoes for us, and we didn't always go without other good food. In the ghetto, most people were malnourished and starving. There'd be no escaping the lice – all ghetto inmates would be infested with lice, she said. And most importantly, she somehow knew, even then, that the ghetto would mean certain death...

When it was liquidated in June 1943, the few people in the Lwów ghetto who'd somehow managed to survive until then were transported to their deaths at the Belzec concentration camp.

So Mama began to make plans. Aunty Rena came with us as her husband, Marek, had fled to Russia with Mania's husband, Bolek. It was considered safer there for men than in Poland at this time. Mama had been in touch with Zayda – I don't know how – maybe a phone call. But anyway, she worked out that Zayda could help us escape from Lwów.

'I've organised a way of getting out of here,' Mama told me and Binka that night. 'There is a man in our building, a friend we can trust, Zayda says. His name is Salek Donsky.'

'But why should we trust him?' Binka said. 'He's a gentile Pole, not a Jew!'

'Zayda has been friends with him for years, Binka. You trust Zayda, don't you? Well then . . . Mr Donsky will pick us up from Lwów, and Zayda will pay him for his service.'

Binka looked as though she didn't believe Mama for a minute.

'Binka! I've said. They have been friends for years. What choice do we have?'

'But it's such a risk, Larissa. A huge risk! You know many Poles give away Jews to the Germans! And I'm sure they all said they've been friends for years too. That doesn't count for anything any more.'

Mama was getting angry with Binka again. She always went silent when she got really angry. Then she added, 'Binka, we do not have a choice. We cannot know completely who to trust. The arrangements are made. You can come with us or stay here.'

That was enough for Binka to change her mind. 'All right. We will trust this Mr Donsky. I pray you are right, Larissa. I pray you are right!'

We packed for our trip back to Brody straight away. I couldn't wait to see Zayda again. For the trip, Mama made sure we had bread and some dark-yellow cheese given to her by one of our gentile neighbours, Mrs Nimsky.

'Oh, she is so kind!' Mama said when she saw the cheese. 'She was always so friendly, and now I know she is so very kind too.'

'Larissa, she doesn't know we are Jews,' said Binka. 'That makes all the difference.'

'I don't care about that. She is kind to people, whatever sort of people they are. Mrs Nimsky got the food from her sister. She has a farm outside Lwów, apparently. How lucky she is! A relative with a farm!'

Mama began packing the bread and cheese, and threw in some tins of sardines too. She seemed cheerful all of a sudden.

'Sasha! Go pack your bag – the grey one with the leather handles. Go! Pack your underwear, and pyjamas and warm clothes. Quickly!'

I went into my bedroom and started to pull some clothes out of the drawers and a warm jacket from the wardrobe. But I didn't care about clothes. I wanted to take more important things. If I'd had a chess set I would've packed that first.

I went over to my bookcase and the two rows of precious books. Some Kipling, and some other English stories, but I was most interested in taking my favourite book, a story called *Kaytek the Wizard* by Janusz Korczak. It'd been given to me by Zayda a few years ago for my birthday. Such a great read – a story about a schoolboy named Kaytek who had magical powers. But he was a troublemaker too, in his home town, so he left and travelled and met a girl who helped him to defeat an evil wizard. It was about growing up, and how Kaytek decided to fight evil rather than join it. That was the story I wanted to take with me.

I put the book in my bag and thought suddenly that the story of Kaytek was a bit like my life now, surrounded by good and evil. But now it seemed to me as though the evil ones were winning. The Nazis were doing terrible things to innocent people. And we were the innocent people – people like Mama and my aunts, Tylda and Zayda and all my friends.

Mama put her head around the door and saw me sitting looking at the book. 'Sasha! Quickly now! Pack your clothes and warm socks. And what on earth are you doing packing your football?' She tossed the ball out of my bag. 'Oh, and where are those things of Bubbe's? Come on, Sasha! We need to go! It's getting dark.'

We had to wait until dark before we could make our way outside. We couldn't risk being seen by anyone who knew us, so we snuck out together, Mama, Binka and me, carrying two suitcases and my smaller leather bag between us. It was cold and a dark night and we waited in the shadows on the street corner, until very soon a man walked up to us and nodded at Mama. It was Mr Donsky.

He said nothing. We just followed him to his car, parked around the corner, and hurried in while Mr Donsky loaded the bags into the boot. I sat in the back between Mama and Binka. Two younger women, one with a little boy on her knee, were sitting in the front seat. They didn't look at us or say anything at all. I thought I should at least say hello, but I was too scared to say anything. Mama was silent, so I was the same.

The car ride back to Brody seemed long and boring. No one spoke, and there was nothing to look at – just the dark night and occasional lights. So I snuggled in to Mama's shoulder and tried to sleep.

It must have been a few hours later – I don't know really – but I was woken by a jolt, and our car slowed down and came to a stop on the side of the road. I noticed the women and the little boy in the front had gone.

Suddenly a large truck forged ahead of our car, but it was stopped by what looked like an official-looking man up ahead. I couldn't see much, but then Mama whispered, 'Polish police! They are talking to the driver.'

Mama looked at Binka and squeezed my hand. 'Oh God, Binka, they are probably transporting Jews.'

The truck was moved on, and the officials approached our car. Mr Donsky talked quietly to them for a few minutes, but then we were moved on too. Mama began breathing again. Binka let out a small sob, and I wondered if that meant we were allowed to go now and that we'd finally arrive safely at Zayda's house after all.

There was more boring travelling through the dark after that, and nothing scary happened. I went back to sleep until I was woken again, this time by Mama. I looked out the window – still dark, but there was a faint hint of light through the trees and the sky was beginning to lighten.

Binka looked at Mama with tears in her eyes. 'Thank God, Larissa, we are home!'

Mr Donsky drove his car up Zayda's drive. I could see the outline of the trees and the garden that Bubbe loved so much, but it somehow looked different. Even in the shadows I could see that it wasn't neat and tidy any more. I couldn't smell any flowers. Perhaps it was the wrong time of year for jasmine and roses. I looked over to where the fruit trees were, in a small orchard Bubbe had planted years before I was even born. I thought of the crunchy apples and delicious pears she'd grown. Her Garden of Eden. But it seemed like the whole orchard was gone. There was an outline of bare trunks and the trees looked more like large dead sticks than living fruit trees. Perhaps Zayda would tell me what had happened to the trees.

The car stopped outside the front porch, and Mama ran to the door and knocked loudly three times. That was the family's knock, a special code she'd organised with Zayda before we left.

The door swung open and I gasped with happiness when I saw Zayda, my beloved grandfather, dressed in a light-coloured dressing gown. Binka and I got out of the car then and saw Mama throw her arms around Zayda, and then he saw me, standing quietly behind Mama on the doorstep.

'Sasha, my boy! My dear boy!' He hugged me close, and we stayed like that for what seemed a very long time. Mama and Binka joined in the hug, and by then I was starting to feel squashed by all the adults. Zayda pushed us apart and kissed me warmly on the cheek.

'You must all be hungry! Come and have some breakfast. We don't have much, but I will warm up some bread in the oven. There is honey for the bread and milk for Sasha. And I managed to find some coffee for my girls – and you too, Donsky!' he said, with a glint in his eye. 'Well done!'

'I will leave you with your family, Richard, but thank you,' Mr Donsky replied. 'Mirka is waiting for me at home.' He quickly said goodbye, but Mama stopped him. 'Thank you for your kindness, Mr Donsky. I will always remember it.'

I thought Zayda looked much thinner than I remembered. He looked tired and his thick dark hair was now silver grey. But I didn't have time to worry about what Zayda looked like. Everybody moved into the sitting room and began talking about what was happening in Lwów, and Zayda told us the news from Brody.

Mama's other sister, Mania, and her daughter, Selena, were also at Zayda's house by now, living in a few rooms of their own upstairs. They hadn't made it to Palestine. The war had begun before they could travel – and now they had Selena who was only three months old.

'Mania and Selena will stay with us for now. We've heard no news from Bolek or Marek since they fled to Russia. We have to hope they are all right, that it will be safer there for them than here in Poland. It is the Jewish men here who are most at risk now.'

'At least we will all be together,' Binka said softly, squeezing her father's hand.

And after breakfast, which I thought was delicious because Zayda had made frothy milk too, he turned to me at last and said, 'Sasha, are we to have a game of chess later?'

'Yes, Zayda! Yes, please! But you know I will beat you again.' I laughed.

'Go and find my chess set then. It is in the usual place.'

I ran out into the hall and found the cupboard where the chess set was always stored. It was a good night, that first night back in Brody. Zayda won the chess game, of course. And for the rest of that first day we all just slept and caught up with more news from Zayda. Dinner was a quick meal of bread and soup, until it was time to sleep again and wait for the next day.

But the morning brought only more bad news.

'My girls, I have something to tell you,' Zayda said after breakfast. 'I should have told you straight away, but there is no easy way...'

Mama looked at me. 'Sasha, go into the other room.'

'But I don't want to!' I protested. I was tired of people thinking I shouldn't know things. I'd already seen enough. I was used to bad news.

'The boy can stay,' Zayda said, and smiled sadly at me. Then he turned to Mama. 'I did not want to write or tell you on the phone, not this news.'

'Papa?'

'Your brother Daniel was killed.'

Binka gasped.

'On a train. Three months ago now. The train was bombed, a huge explosion. He was with his fellow army officers. But he wouldn't have known a thing – he would have died instantly. I am sure of it.'

Binka burst into tears. Mama said nothing and began to scratch her hand and bite her lower lip.

All I could think of at that moment was that Uncle Daniel wouldn't be able to have Zayda's chess set any more.

'Why didn't you let us know earlier?' cried Binka.

'My darling girl, I was worried about getting you *here*! At first I couldn't work out how to keep you safe. It would've been too dangerous for you to come earlier and, even if you'd known earlier, there was nothing you could do.' He sighed.

'Was his body found?' Mama asked.

'No, not found. We were told the whole thing happened very fast.' Zayda lowered his head. He did not want to look at me.

'Why'd he have to join the Polish army?' I asked.

'You know, Sasha,' Zayda said, raising his head to look at me at last. 'He was always close to my brother, Felix, and so he followed him into the army. He wanted to be an officer, just like him. I am proud to say he achieved that goal.' But Zayda's voice sounded sad, not proud.

We sat together in silence around the table. I fiddled with the edge of the tablecloth and for most of the time I just kept my eyes down. Zayda said we should keep a minute's silence and remember Uncle Daniel for a moment.

Then Mama spoke. 'D'you remember, Binka, how Daniel would stand at the door of our bedrooms and toss the feather pillows at us? He had such a good aim! I'd be reading in bed and he'd hurl that pillow at me.'

'Yes,' Binka said with tears in her voice. 'I remember once I was braiding my hair and he threw a pillow at me and I got so angry with him I chased him back to his room.'

'And then we'd all pile in on top of each other and have one great big pillow fight.'

I went to bed that night thinking of pillow fights, hoping that one day soon I'd see Sam and Walter again and that maybe then I would have a pillow fight with them. Better than real fights. Better than real wars.

It took me a long time to get to sleep that night.

Chapter 6
THE BARN

For now, most of our family was reunited and safe. And life wasn't quite as bad in Brody as it was in Lwów. There was no ghetto in Brody yet.

It was pretty crowded though, with all of us crammed into Zayda's house. Sometimes that was good because there was always someone around to talk to, or find a book with, or go out into the garden with. But sometimes Mama got tired, and sometimes she got so tired she didn't want to talk to me or have me around. And sometimes, too, Mama didn't seem to get on very well with Sonia. I thought maybe that was because Sonia was Zayda's wife now, and she'd taken Bubbe's place and Mama was sad about that – Sonia being here instead of her real mama. Kind of filling her shoes.

It turns out I was right about that. One morning when the rest of the family were at the market trying to buy food, I came in from the garden and saw Mama sort of slumped in a chair opposite Zayda. They couldn't see me from where they were sitting, and I didn't like the way Mama seemed so sad.

'I still do not know how you could have done that to us, Papa. Mama had been dead only weeks. And you had to marry again? So soon? It was never fair to her memory. I'm not saying I don't like Sonia, you know I do. But to forget Mama so soon . . .'

'I never forgot her, Larissa. I could not cope without a wife to look after such young children. You are being unfair.'

Mama didn't move.

Zayda got up from his chair, walked over to Mama and took her hand in his. 'Larinka!' he said softly in his quiet voice that he sometimes used with me too. 'I could not run a timber mill and look after five children, five *young* children, all on my own.'

Mama looked at Zayda and I knew she was crying. 'But how? How could you do this, to our mother?'

'I never replaced her, Larissa.'

Then, all of a sudden, Mama seemed to get very angry, and she stood up from her chair and looked Zayda straight in the face. '*No one* will *ever* replace *our mother!*' and she stormed out of the room, slamming the door right near where I was standing.

I'd never seen Mama do something like that before. I didn't wait to see what would happen next. I crept back out to the garden and sat under the old orchard trees, drawing pictures in the dirt. I wished

Mama hadn't taken the football out of my bag when we'd left.

I didn't go back inside until Sonia called me in for dinner.

In the next week Mama amazingly managed to find a one-bedroom flat just for us. It wasn't far from Zayda's, and it had a small kitchen cupboard to cook in, and one bed that I had to share with Mama. We slept top-to-tail, and my feet kept pressing against her head when we slept, but it was cosy and warm and better than sleeping with bombs exploding outside. I missed my own bedroom, but not the bombs.

I knew Mama was happier here. She'd even brought some family heirlooms with her from Lwów – Bubbe's sacred locket, her beautiful bed linen and embroidered tablecloths.

'Mama, why did you bring things like that?' They seemed a bit pointless to me. I thought of my football again.

'We can trade some of the linen for milk and bread, Sasha. Maybe even potatoes and eggs. Whatever the Polish peasants in the villages have near here.' She unpacked the linen, put it aside in a kitchen drawer, and took the locket in her hand. It was shaped like a little heart made of gold, on a long golden chain.

'You won't trade Bubbe's locket, though, will you?'

'No, Sasha. Of course not. Not the locket.' She undid the clasp and put it around her neck. 'This is too special, a part of Bubbe. We must keep it safe to remember her by.'

Whenever we ventured out for food and other things we needed, the women in the village seemed to think Mama was Polish, not Jewish at all. I suppose she didn't look particularly Jewish with her blue eyes and blonde hair and she was fluent in Polish. And anyway, she looked happy because she could find good food here, and Jewish people didn't look happy these days. So we managed to live in Brody peacefully enough for several months.

But then I got sick. It was late autumn by then and the trees were all bronze, red and yellow; the ivy and heather were blooming; and the oak trees were almost bare. I remember those things, but I don't remember how I got sick. I just woke one night with terrible pain in my ear, and smelly pus was oozing out onto the pillow.

'Oh, Sasha!' Mama sighed, frightened. She scrambled off the bed and found a bottle from the kitchen cupboard. She quickly gave me what medicine she had in that, but it wasn't much and she was afraid to call a gentile doctor for fear he would give us away. 'I'll go to Zayda's and phone a Jewish doctor. Zayda will know what to do.'

But when we got to Zayda's and phoned the doctor, he said it was too dangerous for him to come and see me. We'd have to go to Lwów. It might be serious. It might be meningitis. I didn't know what that was, but it frightened Mama and so it frightened me too.

Mama and Zayda didn't have enough money for the train back to Lwów, so Mama had to think fast.

'Come, Sasha, put your coat back on. It's very chilly out there.' She bandaged my head, covering the sore ear, and placed one of Zayda's knitted caps over my head.

Mama thought she might be able to get a lift from one of the trucks that travelled along the main road. We walked for nearly two hours, but nobody stopped. She was getting very worried, but at last one truck did pull over for us. Mama looked inside and saw some Poles. They told her to hop in. My heart was thumping. If they realised we were Jewish they might give us up. But we had no choice. Mama climbed in and pulled me up behind her.

The men in the truck were going into Lwów to sell goods. They were not interested in us. They just talked about business and things I didn't know anything about.

We reached Lwów early the next morning and by then I was in so much pain I was nearly fainting. Mama managed to find the surgery and we were lucky because it wasn't far from where the truck dropped us off. It was Dr Alexandrowicz's, an ear, nose and throat specialist, one of only a few Jews who'd been allowed to keep practising.

Mama rang the bell and a fat blonde woman with rouge painted on her cheeks answered the door. She was dressed in a white uniform and I thought she must be a nurse.

'Can I help you?' she asked.

'I must see Dr Alexandrowicz straight away. I was told to come and see him. My son is very sick!'

'The doctor is busy,' the nurse said.

'But my son is in terrible pain! He has a fever. We've travelled for hours to get here. Please!' Mama begged.

'Wait a moment. I will see what I can do.' The woman in white went away and the doctor came to the door. But his face fell when he recognised us.

'Mrs Fein, I am sorry, but I am not allowed to treat Jews. You will put me and my family in danger.'

'Please, Dr Alexandrowicz, you are our only hope. You are a doctor! You can see he is terribly unwell. Look!' Mama took off my knitted cap and the bandage, which was now stained with pus and very smelly. She bent my head towards the doctor. 'See, there is pus running from his ear. You cannot let us go!'

'I am sorry, Mrs Fein, but you must understand. I have German orders not to treat him.'

Mama changed her voice then, and became calmer. 'Dr Alexandrowicz,' she said. 'Let me ask you one thing before I leave. If you had a boy his age and something terrible like this happened to him, what would you do? Tell me that.'

The doctor hesitated for a few seconds. He did not look at me. 'Come in,' he sighed. 'God knows what will become of us. God knows!'

'Thank you! I will always remember you for what you did for us,' Mama said.

The doctor examined me and cleaned out my ear immediately. But he needed to do it again in a couple of days. If it was left I might get that thing called meningitis.

As he was cleaning my ear, Dr Alexandrowicz suddenly said to Mama, 'You know, I had a boy who would have been about his age now – but he died at birth. Ten years ago it was,' the doctor said, lowering his eyes. He looked as though he was thinking very hard about something. The silence seemed to last a hundred years until he spoke again. 'All right, leave him with me,' the doctor said kindly. 'He is too ill to go anywhere. My wife and I will care for him. I will be happy to help.' Doctor Alexandrowicz gave Mama a phone number and told her to call daily.

'Thank you so much, doctor.' Then Mama turned to me. 'Listen to me, Sasha, I'll call tomorrow and see how you are. Everything will be all right, darling. I'll be back for you.' She kissed me gently on my cheek, but I couldn't see anything much because my eyes were half closed from the pain and I felt hot and dizzy. 'Okay, Mama,' I said, but I was afraid and had no strength left to ask her more.

The days passed slowly when I was at the doctor's. It seemed like weeks before I heard from Mama, but the doctor told me she had rung to see how I was, and that my ear was getting better. I slept a lot, and I woke up afraid because I couldn't remember where I was. I wondered where Mama had gone. I was afraid she wouldn't return. I dreamed about being left in a dark forest, of being lost, and I woke up one night feeling like I'd been pulled awake by something. But I was still in bed, and alone, and I couldn't stop the tears from coming. Why had Mama not come back?

But then one day, it must have been about two weeks later, I don't know, but Mama returned at last to Dr Alexandrowicz's surgery to pick me up.

'How can I thank you enough, doctor!' Mama's face was beaming. She held me so tight that I couldn't breathe. But I felt safe at last.

'Where to now, Mama? Can we go back to Zayda's today?'

Mama didn't answer immediately. She gathered up her bags, then turned to me and said, 'Not quite today, Sasha. We'll stay in Schwabendorf first, where it is safer, and find a place to stay. We won't be far from Zayda.'

I didn't know it then, but Mama wasn't telling me everything that day. Later she did, but when we left the doctor's I had no idea that Zayda had warned Mama a week before that it was getting too dangerous to remain in the city, where Jews were increasingly hunted down and sent to the camps. Zayda had news of an *aktion*, where German soldiers gather up 'undesirables'. We were 'undesirables'. And the *aktion* was spreading wider than he'd originally thought. It might even reach the outskirts of Brody. He urged Mama not to come back.

In fact when I'd been at the doctor's, Mama hadn't gone home at all. She'd stayed with a friend in Lwów, hidden for the whole two weeks I was sick. Some people were so good. Like the doctor and Mama's friends, they took risks to help others. The penalty for non-Jews hiding Jews was death.

'For now, Sasha, we are going to stay with another of Zayda's very dear friends. He is called Mr Krzyinski. You will like him, Sasha.'

'Does he work for Zayda then?'

'Not exactly, no. Zayda gave some work to his sons, to help them through the war. So Mr Krzyinski feels very grateful to our Zayda. It's all about people helping people, Sasha. Mr Krzyinski is not a healthy man now and he cannot work much. His family doesn't have much money. But he will help us – he is a generous man.'

Mama and I left the doctor's house that day and found another truck that would take us back to Schwabendorf. From there we walked to Mr Krzyinski's house on the outskirts of town.

Mr Krzyinski was kind and old and frail, but welcomed us and shared what little food he had. He'd been living mainly on potato cakes made from leftover potato peel that he had saved, so there wasn't much to share really. But I didn't mind. I was better and I was with Mama and we were away from danger.

'A poor diet for a growing, boy, Sasha!' Mr Krzyinski said as he smiled at me and passed me a plate of fried potato cake. 'But what we have we have to share.'

'Thank you, Mr Krzyinski,' said Mama. 'You are very kind.'

'You must be careful though, Larissa. Stay here one night only, or people will catch up with you. There are some farms a little further out of town. I think it better, safer, if you go there. I am sure there will be a barn or two where you can hide for a while, until the *aktion* has passed through this area. We've seen what is happening – rows and rows of Jews being deported.'

'I suppose it is far too dangerous to try and get to Brody straight away.'

'Yes, of course,' said Mr Krzyinski. 'In towns they are rounded up, sent on trains. But here...' And he handed Mama a slip of paper. 'I have drawn you a little map. Of the local farmland. The forests and farmland are safest. And here is a torch you can take, but use it sparingly. The batteries won't last forever.'

'Oh, Mr Krzyinski, you are so kind!' I could see tears in Mama's eyes.

'I am only doing my part. As Mr Hassenstein says, we need to treat people honestly, no matter if they are Jew, or Pole or German.'

I didn't know who Mr Hassenstein was, but Mama said he was an important man in Brody who was helping the Jews avoid the *aktionen*.

We left the following night, just before dark, and headed in the direction Mr Krzyinski told us to go, over towards the farms on the outskirts of town. It was only a short walk compared to the ones I'd had to do lately, and we soon came across a large barn, red with a big wooden door that was crusty with peeling paint and rusty nails.

'Come on, Sasha. Let's get inside and find a nice comfortable place to rest.'

I helped Mama open the barn's big squeaky door, and in the dim light I could see a large area downstairs with some rusty farm equipment stacked in a corner, and an upstairs loft full of hay bales and some old bridles and harness. It smelt of hay, horses, old boots and rope. And something else.

I looked around and clutched my nose. 'Mama, what's that awful smell?'

'Sasha, it's only horse manure, darling. You like horses.'

'Not the smell of manure, I don't.'

'Well, it's not so bad. The main thing is that there is nobody here and we can hide under all this hay. Look how it almost looks like fluffy clouds! Come on. Up the stairs. We will bury ourselves in hay. It will be like an adventure, Sasha! A game of hide and seek.'

I thought the haystack didn't feel anything like fluffy clouds, and it annoyed me when Mama sometimes said ridiculous things like that just to try to make me feel better. It wasn't like any game of hide and seek I wanted to play, not when the people seeking us were Nazis.

The hay up in the loft was itchy and sticking uncomfortably into my skin and clothes, and I still thought it stank. But I was exhausted by now, and we went to sleep almost immediately. I dreamt of horses moving around a giant chessboard, with Zayda shouting instructions.

It must have been in the early hours of the following morning that I was jolted awake by a sudden noise. At first, I didn't know what it was, but then I heard Mama say, 'Quiet! Not a sound, Sasha!'

The noise was the barn door being opened, pushed inwards on its rusty hinges and banging against the barn wall. I could hear voices, men's voices, Germans. They started to shout. I couldn't understand what was being said, but Mama could. Instinctively, I knew I had to be silent. She translated what the Germans said after they left.

'*Vielleicht die Schweine sind in der Scheune! Hans, wir suchen hier. Braun wird sehr glücklich sein, wenn wir einige finden.* Perhaps, those swine are in here. Hans, let's search. Braun will be very happy if we find them.' Nazi soldiers. One had a deep voice. I was terrified.

'*Das ist eine gute idee. Anton, wissen Sie mehr schmutzige Juden werden jeden Tag gefunden.* Good idea, Anton. More and more Jews discovered every day!' The other soldier sounded like he was enjoying this. Mama was right. A game of hide and seek. I could hear the soldiers' boots clunking on the barn floor.

'*Schauen Sie auf der rechten Seite, und ich werde auf der linken Seite suchen.* Look to the right. I'll check out the left,' the one called Anton ordered.

And then we heard the most terrifying sound of all. The sound of footsteps climbing the stairs to the loft. We could barely breathe. They were coming closer. Through the tiny gaps in the hay I could see the Germans' weapons in the dim morning light.

The two soldiers began to prod the hay with their rifles. I closed my eyes tight, and waited to die.

A rifle jab just missed the right side of my leg.

'*Es gibt nichts hier.* Nothing here! Let's go!'

'*Und ich kann nicht jemanden hier finden. Braun wird nicht glücklich sein, dass wir mit leeren Händen zurückkehren. Gehen wir, Hans. Es gibt andere Orte, um die Schädlinge zu suchen.* No one over here either. Braun will not be happy with us returning empty-handed. Let's go, Hans. There are other places to search for this vermin.'

We heard the German boots crunching back through the hay and then the door of the barn shut with another loud squeaky bang. I couldn't believe it. It was a miracle we hadn't been found.

'Well, Sasha, that was a close call,' Mama whispered, trying to sound cheerful. But her voice was shaking and she clung tightly to me.

I couldn't speak. I snuggled up against Mama and

shut my eyes tight and prayed for the men outside to go away.

I could hear a lot of noise outside, from the field around the barn. It seemed very close. After a few moments, Mama got up and peered through a tiny crack in the rotting slats of the barn wall. I climbed over to look too, and from there I saw dreadful things.

There were bodies on the ground. And Nazis standing over them. Many Nazis. They were herding people like animals, old people, Jews, into trucks. Mama and I watched as more were dragged forward. If they caused trouble, and a few tried, they were shot on the spot. There were children too. Boys and girls the same age as me. Some were crying and clutching at their parents.

'Mama, what is happening?'

'The farm. Mr Krzyinski warned us. The *aktion*. The farm is being used as a round-up point for Jews.'

There was a lot of shooting now, screaming and wailing. And all we could do was hide in our barn, huddled together in the hay, too scared to breathe.

This terror raged outside for hours. We lost track of the time. The daylight intensified and then the light in the barn dimmed. After a while came the quiet. Not a sound. The silence was worse than the noise.

We must have slept for some of that day and into the next night. For the following morning there was no one outside, no bodies, no trace of the trucks, nothing.

'Now what do we do, Mama?'

'I don't know, Sasha! Oh, I don't know! Perhaps we should stay, but we can't. There is no food here, no water. We'll have to leave, but we must do it quietly and quickly.'

That evening we crossed the field and hurried through the surrounding forest to a small village. We were not far from Brody now. Mama knew yet another contact, a business associate of Zayda's named Charczuk. I thought Zayda must have known half the country with all the contacts he'd given Mama.

'Mr Charczuk lives not far from where we are now, Sasha. We will head there. I'm sure any friend of Zayda's can be trusted to help us.' It seemed to me as though surviving this war was all about who you knew.

We must have looked awful by the time we knocked on Mr Charczuk's door. We were dirty and tired and I still had bits of straw sticking out of my clothes.

'Larissa! Good God, what are you doing here?' The man who answered the door grabbed us quickly and pulled us inside.

'I have nowhere to run! Father has enough to deal with, with everybody under his wing. We've been hiding in a barn, but it's no longer safe. The Germans were all around it, looking for Jews, rounding them up. Oh God! Oh God!'

'Come in, my dear.' The man called down the hallway. 'Mr Jablonski. Some soup for our friends, please.'

'Oh, thank you. Thank you so much, Mr Charczuk. We've been starving.' Mama was in tears and I just couldn't stop shaking.

Mr Jablonski must have been Mr Charczuk's servant, and he soon appeared carrying some watery pea soup from the kitchen. It was the best soup I'd ever tasted. And I didn't even like pea soup.

That's all I remember from that night. We must have slept. We must have been taken to a loft in another barn close by the house, because that's where I woke up the next day. We must have been told how we could keep hidden and safe for a while. But all these details were a blur to me. I was exhausted.

For now I thought the worst must surely be over. Mama and I could stop running. I was better. And we had a dry safe loft in which to live.

I couldn't have been more wrong.

I knew we had to keep safe, away from the Nazis. What I didn't know was what I would be expected to do to achieve this. Nothing prepared me for what Mama had in mind . . .

PART TWO
THE GIRL

Chapter 7
ZAYDA

The war had been raging for three years. Our barn loft was now our haven. Mama and I had no comfortable mattress, no pillows or eiderdown. There was no running water, no toilet or sink, and no bath. All we had was a bed of straw and a bucket for a toilet, which I hated.

There was only a small window that looked out onto a courtyard and a bleak garden. The loft itself had thick wooden beams coming through the floor and because we were right under the sloping roof there was only a thin layer of wooden slats and plaster between us and the roof tiles. I could often hear birds chirping and scratching nearby, and the room was freezing.

But it was our only safe place. It was our sanctuary from the horrors of the war and we were lucky to have it.

Mama was always frightened for us these days. She could never relax, and she didn't smile much. 'Our safety won't last in here, Sasha,' she said. I watched her wring her hands together and pick at her fingernails. 'They are searching for Jews. Always. If the soldiers stop and find us...'

'What, Mama?'

'You've seen them outside. You've seen what they do. To the boys. They ask all the boys to drop their pants, to see if they are Jews. Your circumcision would give you away, Sasha. They'd see you are a Jew and they would take us away.'

Mama was right. I'd seen the Nazis shoot boys and grown men on the spot or – and I thought this was worse – they took them away. We think they were deported to the Nazi death camps. There were three in Poland that we knew of: Belzec, Sobibór and Treblinka. We didn't know if there were any more.

'I've heard these names, Sasha. Whispered by the women at the market.' Mama would sometimes sneak out of hiding and go to buy potatoes in the morning. But she had to be careful and pretend to be a gentile. 'The women there, they whisper about people being taken away on trains. But I didn't get any details,' Mama said. 'I'm too scared to stay too long in case I attract attention. I know I don't look too much like the other Jewish women, but even so... oh, Sasha! I hate the fear I see in people's eyes!'

I hated seeing the fear in Mama's eyes – I was sick of being afraid all the time. But in the loft I was bored too, stuck in one spot, never any change. I couldn't go outside, ever – Mama wouldn't let me and I knew she was right, but I hated being confined. Some days I slouched against the loft wall, listening to what was happening outside, daydreaming and sleeping, nothing to do and nothing to say. Nothing to eat most of the time either.

'Sasha, you are so listless! I know you are bored, but promise me you won't go outside.'

'I promise, Mama.' And I slouched back against the wall.

I missed my friends still, Sam and Walter. I dreamed of football and the parks and lanes of my old neighbourhood. I missed *running*, moving, kicking. I thought about Sam calling out, 'Goal! *Go, Sasha!*' And I missed Zayda as well and wondered how he was. Did he look even older now? Had he had to leave? I would've loved a chessboard right now – I could sit here and work out how to surprise Zayda with an unexpected 'Check!'

One night I was lying on our straw mattress, which had some blankets folded around the straw bales, and I was thinking of chess and soccer, and I'd dozed off until I was jolted awake by a noise – I didn't know what. There was light shining through the loft window but it wasn't daylight. Something was flickering.

Flames. The pungent smell of smoke wafted through a tiny crack in the window. I struggled up and shook Mama urgently on the shoulder.

'What is it, Sasha?' And then she clutched my arm when she smelt the smoke too, instantly alert.

I nodded towards the window. We heard a scream from outside. Shots. Sounds that always made me tremble. Mama gripped my forearm tightly and pulled me down beside her, a finger to her lips.

Screaming, more shots. Another *aktion*.

The worst part was always the silence afterwards, the lives that had just been snuffed out. Someone's father, someone's mother, or maybe a boy like me. We cowered in our tiny hideout, petrified, listening as the Nazi death squad carried out their work, picking off their prey who were Jews like us.

Outside, we heard running feet and someone screaming again. A soldier's laugh drifted up through the air. Mama hugged me closer, half trying to hide the sound she knew was coming next – another gunshot rang out across the night sky.

This went on for hours. And it was many more hours before we could sleep again, long after the soldiers had passed on. Long after the sounds and the dreadful screaming had stopped. I shivered in the dark, but not just with cold.

Other nights brought different sounds, but just as terrifying – the endless drone of Nazi bombers above us in the sky. One night the noise went on for so long that Mama even took me by the hand and led me outside into the dark because she could no longer stand not knowing what was going on. I think she thought being careful was suddenly pointless. There was so much confusion, people running for their lives in the thick air filled with the smoke from so many bombs. Nearby villages had been hit. We could see flames in the distance. 'It's Brody,' Mama said with tears in her eyes.

We didn't stay outside for long. Mama finally realised the danger and we scurried back inside, being careful no one saw us going in the back door.

From inside we could see bodies, ripped apart by the blasts, strewn across the nearby fields. Some people were still alive. We could hear them groaning, and I could see pieces of flesh against walls or impaled on fences. One woman's face was a mat of scarlet and black. And I will never forget the stench of burning flesh. Death seemed to circle around us. It was only a matter of time ...

One night, a day or two after that night of the bombing raids, Mr Jablonski hammered on our door with three taps, our secret code.

'I have news from Brody,' he whispered. He looked nervous, and shuffled from foot to foot.

My heart was pounding. I was so afraid it would be very bad news, but Mama gestured for him to come in, glancing behind her to check on me. I was supposed to be asleep on the straw pallet. If the news was bad, she didn't want me to hear, so I had got good at pretending to be asleep at times like this.

'I have news of the Feins,' Jablonski said. 'Aaron's mother and father, they have been arrested.'

I heard Mama gasp. Aaron was my papa's name.

Jablonski continued. 'Their friends, and three sisters – Sarelle, Chana and Malka Fishman – all arrested, along with other Jews. Loaded into trains! We do not know where they've been taken.'

I squinted through half-shut eyes so Mama wouldn't know I was awake and listening. I saw her sink into the straw. 'Who else?' she asked. 'Not my family too? Surely not!' She got up and clutched at Mr Jablonski's shirt.

Mr Jablonski spoke kindly but tried not to look at Mama. 'Your stepmother and sisters are safe.'

'Oh, thank God!'

Mr Jablonski said nothing more.

'And my father?' asked Mama.

Not Zayda, I prayed desperately. Not Zayda! I didn't like the way Mr Jablonski had gone quiet.

He eventually spoke. 'Your father... I am sorry... he was captured. We believe he was taken to Belzec.'

Mama's body seemed to stiffen then and she fell to her knees once more. I think she knew, and I knew too, just at that moment. We knew we would never see Zayda again.

'Do you know if he is still there?'

Mr Jablonski seemed to hesitate again. 'I have... news. I'm not sure how much you want to know, Larissa.'

'Go on... please...'

'There is only a little more to tell. A miracle really that we have any news at all. From an acquaintance, Larissa, someone who knew your father. Somehow he escaped the camp, and brought news of loved ones back to relatives. He said people at the camp – inmates – had to hand in money or valuables. He said your father did not hand in a gold-plated pocketknife.'

Mama gasped again. Mr Jablonski went on.

'But the guards checked him in the line, and they found the knife in the pocket of his trousers.'

'And?'

'I am sorry, Larissa. They say... they made an example of him. I cannot say any more.'

'Because you do not know or because you do not want to tell me?'

Mr Jablonski looked away.

'Please...' Mama went on, 'if you know *anything*, you must tell me.'

Mr Jablonski's face screwed up. 'The SS soldiers, they kicked him in the ribs, then his face. He fell to the ground. His nose was broken. I do not know... they say the soldiers were clapping and cheering.'

Zayda! I screamed inside my head. I felt a surge of heat through my whole body and sweat trickled down my forehead. I tried to comprehend that my beloved grandfather could really be dead. I wanted to cry, but tears would not come.

After Jablonski left I could not pretend to be asleep any longer.

'Mama?'

'Sasha! Oh, Sasha!' Mama came over to me and we hugged each other tight for a long time, crying, saying nothing.

Mama began to scratch her right hand, rubbing until she saw droplets of blood. She looked down at her stained hand and seemed confused and unable to move. I sat watching her until at last she spoke.

'Sasha, you look so thin. You are famished and I haven't even noticed. Your cheeks, they are sunken now. And look at your bones.'

It was true – I was a lot thinner than I'd ever been before.

'Sasha, you are just a fairer version of your father. He was sensitive, just like you. His lips used to quiver whenever he felt sad or angry!' She hugged me tighter and the tears ran down her cheeks. 'He was taller, but then you are still only young. And yet the spark in your lovely blue eyes – it is fading fast. This dreadful war! I fear more watery pea soup from our protector Mr Jablonski and Mr Charczuk will not sustain us much longer. They barely have enough for themselves.'

I lay back in Mama's arms and thought of Zayda. I wondered what his last moments were like. I wondered if he thought of me, of our chess games. Or whether he'd been so frightened he hadn't been thinking of anything at all. He'd found out what it was like to die, how it felt not to be here any more.

So I just lay there now, in Mama's arms, not wanting to move any more. I wondered what my last moment on earth would be like, what I'd think of. Maybe my family. Maybe what I'd miss out on, things like kissing a girl, which Sam always bragged about, having a family of my own one day maybe. Would I think about all that? About how I'd missed out on a future career? I thought of the Lwów mathematicians from the Scottish Café. I thought of Papa. He'd been a lawyer. Maybe I would've been a businessman like Zayda. Zayda, what were you thinking in the moments before you died?

I couldn't know it then, of course, what Zayda had been through. I couldn't know of the dreadful things he'd been spared from because he'd been one of the first to die in that camp. But later I knew, and I felt thankful that he hadn't lived long enough. Not long enough to see the women and young girls shorn like lambs, stripped naked and led to the showers of death to be gassed. He did not see those who walked in silence, prayed or wept as families huddled together and climbed up the wooden stairs that led to their final end. He knew nothing of gas chambers. He did not see their bodies covered in sweat, urine, blood and excrement, tossed outside like garbage. And he didn't see the Nazis force the mouths of the dead open with iron hooks to remove gold fillings from their teeth. He did not see, either, the bodies thrown into a large ditch near the gas chamber, splashed with diesel oil and burnt. He saw no mass graves, no three-year-old children buried alive in cold bare pits. Zayda, my dear Zayda, never heard their last cries as the dirt fell over their tiny innocent heads.

Chapter 8
DESPERATE MEASURES

I was growing up. I was scrawny and malnourished, but still getting taller, and I didn't feel like a little kid any more. Sam and Walter would be taller now too, more like the older boys at school. I felt sick sometimes, thinking about all this, thinking about girls, looking at the weird changes in me. I had to put up with developing into a man without a papa, without the usual family traditions. And worst of all, Mama wanted to *talk* about it. I wish she'd just forget about growing up. All I wanted to do was to be ignored.

'It's very sad for you, Sasha, missing out on a normal boyhood. I wish your papa was here now for you. You need a papa, to explain things . . . about girls and about –'

'For God's sake, Mama!' We'd just woken up and were lying head to feet on the straw bed. At least I couldn't see her eyes from where I was.

'Well, it's true! You are nearly thirteen. You'll be a young man soon.'

'I'm fine.'

'One day you will meet a girl and –'

'Not much chance of that in here, Mama.'

'Well, one day.'

I lay in the dark, hoping Mama would change the subject. But she kept on about girls.

'One day you will experience . . . young love.'

'Mama!' I groaned.

A line of light crept into the loft from the narrow window. It was almost dawn. Another day with nothing to do. I wished Mama had more to do. It might stop her from wanting to talk about embarrassing things.

'You know, Sasha, I watch you sleep sometimes. You look so pale these days. Your skin doesn't even look like olive skin any more. You are too sallow. You haven't seen the sun enough. Vitamins, you need more vitamins. It can't be good for you, all this being inside.'

'Mama, we can't do anything about it.'

'Oh, Sasha! Your father is dead, your grandfather too, you cannot even kick a football safely in the open air! But . . .'

Mama suddenly sounded angry and determined. Not that she could do anything, I thought.

'Well, I can tell you this, Sasha! Your grandfather's fate will *not* be yours! I *will* not let this happen to my son! I will never, *never* allow you to be captured.

I will never see you dead in a concentration camp!'

'Mama, stop it. Please!'

'But what can I do?'

'Nothing, Mama. I am fine.'

'We need help, Sasha. I have to think of someone who can help us.'

'There is no one, Mama.'

'There is one person who might help. I was thinking...'

'Who?'

'Sasha, you remember Mrs Kolsky?'

'What? My teacher!'

'Yes, your Polish teacher. She loved you so much. And I know she lives nearby... if she still lives nearby.'

'But it's ridiculous, Mama! How could she help? She's probably not even here any more.'

'Well, there is only one way to find out. I will go to her old house today. Ask for Mala Kolsky and say I am a friend. If she's there she will do anything to help you, Sasha.'

I thought the whole idea was stupid. I had no idea what Mama was thinking. But that morning she crept out of our loft, and left me to sleep. I didn't know when she'd return or how long it would take to find my old teacher, or if that was even possible. I didn't want Mama to go. I was afraid of her not coming home. I remembered the days in Lwów when she'd go to work and I was so little I cried because I thought she wouldn't come back.

It was late in the day when I woke and found Mama had returned.

'Well? Did you find my teacher, Mama?'

'I did, Sasha.'

'Really? What did she say? Can she help?'

'I think so, but I need to see someone else first. I will go tomorrow.'

'Again!' I said. 'Why d'you have to go again?'

'Mala has given me a name. Someone who might help. Just be patient. We'll know more tomorrow. Tomorrow I will go to Brody.'

'Brody! It's too dangerous to go to Brody. You said so yourself.'

But Mama wasn't going to listen. All she said was that she'd been given a name. And she was going tomorrow.

The next morning she tied a scarf over her head to conceal her face a little. If she was spotted and recognised . . . Nazi soldiers were everywhere. It was extremely dangerous out there.

Mama came back again, late in the day just as she had the day before, and said nothing about where she'd been or what she'd done. She was tired and out of breath when she returned.

'There has to be another way to get help, Mama. This is silly. You won't tell me anything.'

'I was thinking about your childhood today, Sasha, about how idyllic it was, those outings with Tylda to the Scottish Café! Remember?'

I thought of our house and garden back in Lwów. Of my bedroom. Of Tylda and Binka and Sam and Walter. 'Won't you tell me your plan, Mama? What are you doing, going out all the time?'

'Give me a little more time and I will explain everything. Now, I have to act quickly.'

It was late the following morning, and the sun was hiding behind the clouds. I woke up, feeling groggy. I was used to this feeling of weakness now and had almost forgotten what it felt like to be healthy and full of energy.

There were three taps at the door. It meant it was lunchtime. Mr Jablonsky brought in some pea soup and left in a hurry to get on with his chores. Mama was putting on her headscarf, getting ready to go out yet again. I watched her tie the scarf over her head and around her neck. She'd forgotten to put on Bubbe's locket today, I noticed.

'Mama, where are you going this time?' I hated being left alone in the loft. 'Do you really have to leave – again?'

'Darling, I must. Just wait here patiently. I have to find a way out for us.'

'Well, take me with you this time. Please, take me with you.'

'It's too risky, Sasha. Be patient, and I will work out how we can escape,' she said, hugging me tight. 'I'll be back very soon, I promise.' She kissed me and left once more.

These trips of Mama's went on for days, I don't know exactly how many – a week maybe – but every time she came back and told me nothing. And every time she would say she'd tell me soon. Until one day. It is the one day I will never forget.

I was in our loft, of course, just pacing up and down because Mama had been away a very long time that day and it was getting dark. I hated being left alone, but after dark was worse. I was more than usually worried that day because she'd taken so much longer than usual. Then suddenly the door opened and she was there. She was smiling, but I just whirled around and glared at her. 'Where have you been for so long? I thought you'd been caught, Mama!' I was nearly in tears.

'Oh, Sasha! I am sorry! Really I am, but look!' she said excitedly. She had a package with her, and began unwrapping it. 'I brought you something to eat.'

I leant towards the package and peered inside the brown paper wrapping. I could see potato skins. 'Where did you get this?'

'I went to see my friend, Marysia Gruzinski. She gave them to me. Come and eat, and I will tell you all about it.'

I jumped at the potato skins, devouring them as fast as I could. I stopped being so angry with Mama and began to feel less ravenously hungry as my empty stomach soaked up the salty sliced potato.

'So, Sasha! I have a plan! A great plan for us! It is a long story, and I must tell you right from the start. This is how I did it.'

'Did what?'

'Saved us, Sasha. Saved *you*.'

'What?'

'Your Polish teacher, Mala Kolsky – she gave me the name of a priest.'

'A *priest*?'

'Yes, don't sound so shocked, Sasha. A priest in Brody, in a church not twenty minutes from here.'

'Is that where you've been going?'

'Partly. At first I couldn't find him, but eventually I did, and we spoke, in secret, behind the curtain of a confession box. Think of it, Sasha! Me in a confession box! It was very strange. I've never been in a confession box before.'

'Of course not, Mama! We're Jewish.' I thought this was ridiculous.

'But the priest, he was very kind. I told him we were fleeing the Nazis. That we were Jews. Mala said I could trust him. And he listened very carefully and said he could help us. Oh, I was so grateful!' Mama was almost crying by now, but she continued with her story.

'He said he could give us documents to say we were Catholics.'

'What?'

'But of course we'd have to learn the catechism, be baptised, convert to Catholicism. He even passed a Bible to me through the curtain. But I didn't know what to do. I felt sick! Like my heart might explode. How could we renounce our own religion?'

I immediately thought of Zayda. What he taught me about God and the Jews, of gentiles and the Enlightenment. I thought of the *yiddishkeit* he fostered in his home. I saw the silver candlesticks Mama would light on the Sabbath at our Friday night dinners in Schwaby. I could hear instantly Zayda's voice reciting the blessing. I could smell the *challah* baking in the oven and almost taste the chicken, sprinkled with salt and pepper, roasted with garlic and bay leaves. The fresh white table linen and Bubbe's finest dishes, crystal glasses filled with red wine. The laughter of our family. How could we be anything but Jewish?

Tears began to roll down my face. Where was our God now, the one I was raised with, the one who was supposed to be always here, generation after generation, to guide and lead? That's what Zayda had said. I was a Jew, born and bred.

But Mama was continuing with her story.

'And of course I told the priest I could do no such thing. It was unthinkable. Becoming a Catholic. But then he asked did I know Marysia Gruzinski. Remember, Sasha? Our kind Polish friend who lived next door? He knew her. She was a gentile, he said, who would help us. And Marysia had a daughter called Sala.'

Now I was wondering where all this was going. 'Mama, I don't understand what this has got to do with us being saved from the Nazis. So we are not going to become Catholics then? And how did the priest know we'd know Mrs Gruzinski anyway?'

'Mala had told him where we lived.'

I remembered Mrs Gruzinski only a little. She'd lived nearby when I was only small. Mama used to visit her. I remembered the smell of fried onions wafting from her house and the sizzle of oil in a pan as she prepared *pierogi* for dinner. Funny that I almost always remembered food these days. My mouth began to water. I could almost taste it! And Mama's sweet succulent *kugel*, made with jam stacked with tiers of macaroni. And chocolate cake, layered with homemade biscuits, chocolate melting and dripping between the layers. In wartime, in our loft, food had become my fantasy.

I forced myself to listen to what Mama was saying.

'So after I left the priest I went to Marysia's old house, Sasha. Oh, I remember it so well. Those tall blackthorn trees. They used to look magnificent when they were covered in creamy white blossoms. But last week when I hurried past, all I could do was watch out for soldiers.'

'Did you find her, Mama?'

'Yes! Yes, I did. And I explained everything to her, Sasha, where we were hiding, how dangerous it is for us. I told her I had to save you. I had no more options left. I needed her help.'

'But she can't hide us, Mama! She'd be found out too, for hiding Jews. If she was caught she'd be shot.'

Mama went pale and her hands trembled. She began to speak again, but this time in a very steady and serious voice.

'I did not ask her to hide us, Sasha.' Mama stiffened her back. She knew as well as I did that asking Mrs Gruzinski to hide us would put her friend in real danger.

'Then what did you ask her?'

Mama looked away and went suddenly quiet.

'Mama?'

'I asked her for papers, Sasha. Identity papers, passports – the papers for Marysia, and for her daughter as well.'

I was very confused by now. 'Well, you could use Mrs Gruzinski's papers but her daughter's papers won't be much use to me, will they?'

Mama looked at me and said very quietly. 'Well . . . I don't know about that. Sala is about the same age as you.'

I looked quickly at Mama, suddenly afraid. Then she looked up and her eyes met mine. 'So, that is it, Sasha, my boy. Our plan. I have false identity papers from Marysia Gruzinski, for both of us. We are going to pretend to be them. I will be Marysia. And you . . .'

I stopped eating. I felt sick. What was Mama talking about? What she was saying? It didn't make sense.

'You, Sasha, will be her daughter, Sala.'

I just stared at her. She looked straight back at me again. Then she said simply this: 'Dearest Sasha, you are going to become a girl.'

Chapter 9
HOW TO BE A GIRL

The truth was if I'd been a girl, then it would have been far easier for Mama to keep me safe. There would be no risk of the SS soldiers pulling down my trousers and checking to see if I was circumcised. But still, I couldn't believe what Mama was asking me to do.

'Mama, you must be completely mad!' I leapt up and paced around the room.

'Sasha, look at what is happening out there! You know I am right! The SS will not ask Sala, a girl, to drop her trousers. We now have Aryan papers. They say who we are.'

'We are who we are!'

But Mama would not listen. 'The passports have no photographs. They are just documents. And I don't look Jewish. And neither will you – as a girl with blue eyes and blonde hair. This is how we can survive, Sasha.'

'But I'm not a girl! I can't *be* a girl.'

'Of course you can! You *must*.' She reached out a hand to me, but I pushed it away and just stared at the wall. I felt tears beginning.

'This is your chance to live. It is our last hope, Sasha.'

'I can't do it. I can't be a girl! I just can't.'

'All right. Maybe I *am* mad. But we need Aryan papers, and you have a far greater chance of surviving as a girl. As a boy your life is hanging by a thread. But as a girl . . .' Mama was pleading with me by now.

'How are we going to get way with it? I don't even look like a girl!'

'I just have to make it work, that's all. I just have to! And, anyway, it is done now. The deal. I have the papers.'

'How? What do you mean? What deal?'

'Marysia exchanged them. I have paid . . .'

'But we have no money. How could we pay?'

'Not money. Things.'

'What things?' And then I remembered. With a dreadful, heart-wrenching shock I remembered. 'Oh, Mama! Not Bubbe's locket!'

Mama's eyes filled with tears. 'I had no choice, Sasha. It was the most valuable thing I had. And Marysia agreed.'

'But Bubbe's locket!'

Mama calmed herself then. 'I am sure, Sasha, that our beloved Bubbe would have wanted me to exchange her lovely gold locket for a chance at saving her grandson.'

I stared at her. I couldn't believe Bubbe's locket was gone.

'Now, let us look at these papers and have something to eat. And then we will work out a plan.' Mama took a small cardboard box from under her coat, opened the lid and let out a breath of relief as she clutched the papers tightly in her hand. Then she suddenly cheered up. 'And before I left Marysia she offered me some of her hot fried potato to eat! Not skins. Real whole potatoes. She wrapped them up in here, and gave us a little extra, especially for you, Sasha.'

We sat on the floor and ate in silence. After a few bites, I felt the pangs of hunger begin to go away, and I even enjoyed the swirls of oil splashed in my mouth from the cold fried potato. The feeling of having food inside me was so rare it felt almost painful.

'On the way home just then, Sasha, you know,' Mama began, 'I passed two elderly neighbours of ours, and I am sure one of them recognised me. I overheard her say, "Isn't that the Jewish lady who lived around the corner?" But, thank God, I am in this ragged, oversized dress, and I don't think she thought it was me in the end.'

I was sweating a little by now, and my stomach gurgled loudly because it wasn't used to the rich food. I felt a wave of nausea pass over me, at the stress of what had just happened. At the thought of pretending to be a girl. It was a ridiculous, completely far-fetched plan as far as I could see. Stupid. But Mama was right – it was a shot at life.

My heart was thumping. 'Mama, I don't *know* about being a girl. I only know you, Aunt Mania, Binka and Rena. I know that you cook and run the home. I know that you are emotional, and you fight and scream at each other, then kiss and forgive. I know that you . . . bleed once a month and have babies and all that.' Then I stopped and didn't know what else to say. I was nothing like a girl!

But Mama was determined. She knew that turning me into a girl wasn't going to be easy. It would require planning and practice. I would have to really think of myself as a girl and act accordingly. I'd need some inner sense of being female, believe for a period of time that I *was* a girl. I'd have to change the way I dressed, the way I spoke, and everything about my behaviour. There was no other way. Either I became a girl, or I would die.

I looked at Mama again. She sat motionless on the floor, as if frozen. Then she spoke quietly. 'The Nazis have killed your grandfather now, Sasha, and we will be next. You need to understand how desperate we are. Think of Zayda. Think of what he'd say to you. It is only a matter of time before we are found.'

I could feel the blood drain from my face. I stared out through the window of the loft. Darkness surrounded us. I was silent for what seemed like a very long time. And then I wept as I thought of Zayda. And I could not stop. I began to wonder where Zayda's God was now. I'd known that other Jews were being killed, of course I did, but somehow I never thought – never really thought – that it would happen to us. I couldn't picture my own smiling grandfather, my beloved Zayda, being killed. It was impossible. Until today I'd thought I couldn't get any more scared, but now I didn't know... I was terrified of being found out by the Nazis, but I didn't want to be a girl.

I wanted to cuddle up to Mama there on the floor. She kept silent, hoping, I suppose, that I'd begin to see that I had no other choice. She didn't try to convince me any more.

The following morning, Mr Jablonski came and told us that we had to leave. Immediately.

Word was out. German soldiers were coming. And they were searching everywhere. They were looking for Jews in hiding.

Mama wasted no time at all. She pulled out our two small suitcases and began to pack. There wasn't much to get together. Mama only had a few dresses, two pairs of shoes, some underwear and a hairbrush. There were some household things left – Bubbe's embroidered tablecloths and matching napkins, which we hadn't yet been able to exchange; some silver cutlery and one or two small crystal vases Mama had kept aside in case she needed them to barter with. And, of course, there was my precious book about the magician.

I watched her pack my clothes. Except she didn't pack my clothes – no trousers or boys' clothes at all. 'We won't take any of those, Sasha, in case we are stopped and asked questions.'

I looked at her, horrified. 'What do you mean? No one will look in my suitcase. Why would they? I'll look like a girl. They wouldn't have any reason...' I was angry now, as well as afraid, and hated everything.

'I am not taking any chances, Sasha! No discussion! Binka left some of her underwear with me and that will fit you better than mine. Here, you can wear these.' She held up some girls' underpants and what I recognised as one of Aunty Binka's old frocks. Aunty Binka had left it in her wardrobe the day we fled Lwów, but Mama was about the same size so she took the dress, not wanting to waste anything, especially articles of clothing.

I stared at the dress, then at the underpants, and glared at Mama.

'Oh, come on, Sasha! It's just underwear and a dress. You either wear them or you die!'

'Mama!' I could not believe she'd said that to me. She was making me feel even more frightened.

'I am sorry, Sasha, but the time for being gentle with how I say things is over. Put them on.'

I took the underwear and the dress and turned my back to Mama. I began to slide off my old trousers and unbutton the dark blue shirt I'd been wearing almost constantly.

I held the dress up in front of me. A dress! A girl's thing!

I wasn't sure whether to put it on over my head or step into it. I undid the belt and tried to step into it at first, but then I couldn't get it over my chest and get my arms into the sleeves. Mama turned, her impatience showing. 'Oh, for goodness sake, Sasha! Undo the buttons first and put it on over your head.'

The dress was loose. It felt like a tent and I stood there feeling stupid. Then, noticing the belt was still undone, I pulled it in a little and tried to fit it around my waist.

'I hate this, Mama.'

'I know you do. I hate it too, and if we had another solution I would grab it with both hands. But,' she started to say something else and then stopped, looking down at the floor. 'Here, put these on as well.'

Mama tossed me a pair of flat black leather shoes.

'Are these Binka's, too?'

'No. Mine.'

'They're too big.'

'They are all we have. Put socks on first. They will add padding. It will be fine.'

She picked up my trousers and shirt and threw them into a bag. 'These go in the bin,' she said, and she took them outside. I felt every nerve in my body protesting against this. I would crumble at any minute. I was screaming inside. I was scared and angry and fragile. But Mama's calmness, the indifference she seemed now to take towards me was even worse. It didn't matter what I felt any more. She just got on with it. And I was simply expected to do as she said.

Once I'd done up the laces on the black leather shoes, Mama searched through the last remaining pile of clothes and found an old knitted cap, greyish-brown with small flowers embroidered around the edge. She pushed it down over my head, tidying my hair underneath it and making sure some of my blond curls draped around my face. I didn't say a word. I couldn't even look at her. Mama cupped my face in her hands and forced me to look into her eyes.

'I'm sorry, my darling. You must see this is the only way. I promise you, this will work! This is how you will survive.'

Mama seemed to examine my face more closely. 'Your hair has grown long, Sasha. That is good. It is like a curly bob. But I think . . .'

'Think what?'

'We will need a part line, to make you look more feminine. People will notice this if you take off your cap.' Mama went back to her suitcase and took out a small tortoiseshell comb. She took the cap off and began to run the comb through my hair, parting it on the side and making it look a little tidier. I felt like a dog being groomed.

'Yes, just like a girl. Just like a girl!' Mama sounded pleased.

But the hair wasn't the hard bit, and neither was the dress. The worst was still to come.

Mama stood back and eyed me up and down. 'That will do. Now we have to get you to behave like a girl.'

'Mama! This is stupid! Can't I just *look* like one? I'll shut up and never talk to anyone. I won't do or say anything. I promise! I won't have to act like a girl then.'

'Don't be silly, Sasha. You will learn how to move naturally and look comfortable. With my help you can do it. Now, here is how you will walk . . .'

'For God's sake, Mama!' There was no way I was going to do stupid girl walks.

'You can make this easy, or you can make this much more complicated. You have a choice. I suggest you try and make this as easy as possible and cooperate.'

Mama didn't even sound like the same Mama any more. She sounded like the teacher everybody at school hated. I thought again of Sam and Walter, and vowed they would never *ever* find out about me dressed in a dress.

'Now come on, Sasha. There is no time to lose. Watch me! This is how you walk like a girl. Stand straight. Hold your head high, don't slouch, shoulders back. Girls are taught good posture, and they like to look elegant.' Mama began to walk up and down in front of me. I watched for a minute and tried to copy what she was doing.

'Look straight ahead, Sasha. Hold yourself up!' Mama spotted my book lying on the top of the things she'd packed and grabbed it. 'Put this on your head and walk straight. We are doing this until you get it right, my boy. Or I should say, my girl. And I will call you Sala from now on. We must both get used to a new name.'

I didn't say anything, but the book felt weird on my head and it was hard to balance it there and keep straight at the same time. Many times Mama stopped me when I wobbled too much and the book dropped to the ground. 'Try again, Sala!' she said in frustration. 'For goodness' sake, every girl can do this! You should be able to! Come on...' and she put the book back on my head and made me walk up and down again, backwards and forwards, for a long time until I could do it without letting the book fall.

'Excellent, darling! Very good. You are walking beautifully. Now, let's work a little on how you will talk.'

'Mama, I can't.' I was crying by now and so exhausted. I began to think it would be easier just to die. But Mama continued relentlessly.

'Now, you know, Sasha – I mean Sala – in Polish our verbs are gender-based. And of course you have never had to worry about how girls say their verbs.'

'But I've been using boy verbs all my life, Mama. I can't learn girl verbs now.'

'You can and you will. I will help you.'

It was like the worst kind of school exam – in this one if you failed your life was at stake. And how long would it go on for? Weeks? Months? Years? How long would I have to be a girl? When could I be me again? Would I be much older when I finally got to be me? Fifteen? Twenty? I'd never felt so terrified of the future before.

Mama quickly began to talk me through my first grammar lesson as a girl.

'We will start by speaking to each other. As a boy, Sasha, you would ask, *Gdzie ty byles?* Where were you? But now as Sala you have to ask, *Gdzie ty bylas?* See how it works. As a boy, you would ask *Co ty zrobiles?* What did you do? As Sala, you will ask *Co ty zrobilas?* Remember the 'e' becomes an 'a' in your pronunciation. It's very simple. But you *must* remember! It will become a strong part of your female identity from now on.'

I didn't want a female identity. I liked my own identity. But I whispered the feminine verb forms, repeating them after Mama, not really knowing what I was doing, my head numb, unable to concentrate. At least the speech seemed easier than the walking, and I had a good ear for sounds, so after a little while I was beginning to get it. *Gdzie ty bylas?* These were my first words, spoken as a girl.

'Sala, that's very good indeed! And your voice sounds like a girl's still. Thank goodness it hasn't broken yet.'

Sala. My new name. How would I ever get used to it? I wanted Sasha back instantly – everything about the new name made me recoil against it. I wondered how on earth I was going to be convincing as a girl once my voice did get deeper. I thought I'd sound ridiculous.

Church of St Elisabeth in Lwów

Grand Theatre, Lwów, where the ballet and opera were held

Smolka Place, Lwów

Sasha's parents, Larissa and Aaron Fein, at their wedding

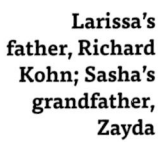

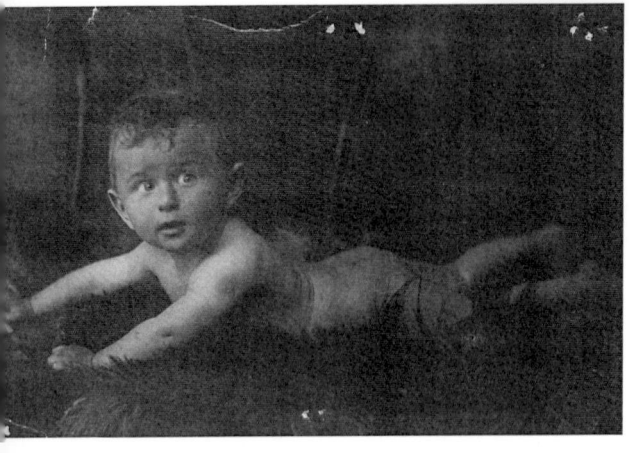

Larissa's father, Richard Kohn; Sasha's grandfather, Zayda

Sasha as a baby

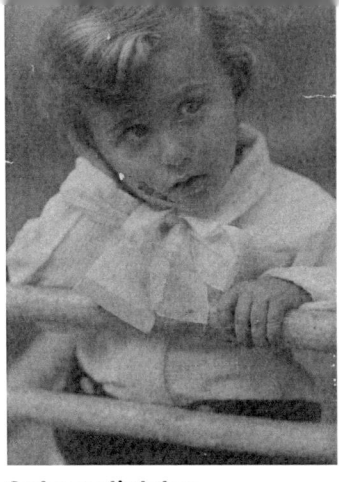

Sasha as a little boy

Sasha and his nanny, Anna

Larissa and Sasha when he was six

Bella Kowalski

Mania and Bolek

Sasha as Sala in Lwów, 1944, aged fourteen and a half

Sasha/Sala (*left*) and Binka (*back*) with two girls from the Lwów apartment building

Lwów train station after the war

Top left–right: Sasha, Misha, Alan and Wicek. *Bottom left–right:* Larissa, Binka and her baby girl Amelia, Selena, and Rena (Larissa's sister married to Wicek)

Sasha and Wicek in Munich after the war

Left, top and below: Sasha and Mila on the *Surriento*

Sasha and Mila at their wedding

Mila, the author as a baby and Larissa

Larissa and the author as a little girl

Entries from Larissa's memoir

Father's Day card from the author to her father, Sasha, and a photograph of them

That morning Mama and I hurriedly practised phrases together, learning to say, 'I went', 'I am afraid', 'I am hungry' and 'Help me'. I said the words after Mama, repeating them endlessly, feeling numb and stupid.

'Okay, my darling. That is very good progress. It will be enough for now. We will practise more in time. Once we are outside again, just remember, don't speak unless you absolutely have to. If you get stuck, just look at me and I will help.'

Mama did not tell me where we were going. But that afternoon we packed up our last few things and left the loft together for the last time. And I was wearing a dress.

Chapter 10
BACK TO LWÓW

We headed for the train station. I guessed then that Mama was planning to get us back to Lwów. I had to ask her just to be sure, and I thought maybe she had plans that she hadn't finished working out yet.

'Mama, where are we going?'

'To Bella. She will help us.'

So we *were* going home, sort of. Back to Bella and Lwów and our beautiful town of cafes and parks.

The trip was supposed to take two hours, but it ended up taking a whole day. There were bombings along the way, and the train had to make many stops. For the entire journey, agonising hours of it, I sat close to Mama, staring at the carriage floor, hoping no one would speak to us or ask us to move. I hated moving in this dress. I felt so uncomfortable and I was so self-conscious. I thought someone would soon get suspicious and discover I was really a boy.

The SS came through the carriages after only a few hours, looking for Jews. Jews like us with false papers.

'Don't worry, Sala,' Mama whispered. 'We're sitting

with our Polish friends, look. They will not worry about us. We are not Jews.' She smiled at me and I hugged her arm. Miraculously, we were never questioned. She was right – we didn't look Jewish enough.

At the Lwów railway station things looked scary, and I stayed as close to Mama as I could. There were police everywhere here, SS, always searching for people with false papers. Ours were firmly tucked away in Mama's bag, so we kept our heads down and scuttled past, trying to look as though it was just another day for us. I did my best to copy how Mama walked and hoped I looked like the other girls in dresses as we walked past. Other girls. Me, now among them.

'Walk on ahead, Sala, while I get our suitcases.'

'But, Mama, no!'

'Just wait here, Sash . . . Sala. It is fine.'

I did as I was told, but I was terrified I would be stopped and interrogated by one of the SS officers. The Gestapo was patrolling the entire station. If I were asked anything I wouldn't even be able to speak, let alone sound like a girl. I knew I'd give us away. We'd be hauled away to the camps. But before I knew it Mama was back at my side with our two suitcases. We didn't turn around or look to see who was near. We took a suitcase each and walked briskly out of the station.

Bella now lived about fifteen minutes' walk from the station. When we got there, I hovered behind Mama as she rang the bell. Then suddenly there was Bella opening the door and looking completely surprised.

'Larissa! Oh, Larissa! Larissa! How on earth are you here? And Sasha –'

I stepped out from behind Mama – and Bella let out a sharp gasp of surprise.

'Oh Jesus Maria! What on *earth* is this?' Bella looked at Mama for an explanation. 'Sasha, in a dress?'

'I will explain. I will explain, Bella. Only, please, can we come in straight away?'

'Yes, of course, of course. Come in! Come in! I cannot believe it is you.'

Mama fidgeted with her handbag, and Bella hurried us into the hallway, a constant look of confusion on her face. I thought Bella looked older now, worn out and thin, just like Mama – it was the toll of war. But I knew she was thinking what on earth was I doing dressed in a girl's frock? And probably wondering why we'd risked coming to Lwów at all when the SS were murdering Jews all around us.

'Oh, Larissa!' Bella said once we were in the living room, and she hugged her tight. Mama and Bella didn't need words to understand each other. They were such close friends. Like sisters. Just a look in the eye was enough. Zayda always said to me – it didn't matter what religion people were. Bella was Catholic and Mama was a Jew. Friendship was all that mattered. But Hitler would never see that. He hated us. To him we were inferior. He loved only Aryans.

'Oh, Bella, we are cut from the same cloth, we are. It is so good to see you. It is so good to know you are safe!'

We sat down on Bella's sofa and it was only then that Bella openly stared at me, completely dumbstruck. She turned to Mama and shook her head in disbelief. 'Why, Larissa, why on earth is Sasha wearing a *dress*?'

Mama began to explain her plan, and all Bella could do was stare in astonishment and open her mouth wider and wider as Mama went on.

'Jesus Maria!' she blurted out again. I thought Catholics must say that a lot. 'Larissa, you are a genius! Isn't she a genius, Sasha? Thinking of such a brilliant plan. Fancy turning a young boy like you into a girl!'

That wasn't the reaction I was expecting. I was hoping Bella would say it was a stupid idea and that I should take the dress off straight away.

'Tonight you'll stay here,' Bella continued. 'Get a good night's sleep. We'll talk about what's to be done in the morning. Come on, I'll show you to your bedroom. I have only one but you'll be warm and safe and it is quiet here.'

I wanted so much to be left by myself that night, but I'd have to share a bed with Mama. Bella showed us into a large comfortable room, with a double bed over by the wall, covered with an eiderdown encased in beautifully crisp white linen and clean fresh sheets. I couldn't believe it. I hadn't seen a proper, comfortable bed with white sheets like this for a very long time. I forgot about having to be a girl, ran straight to the bed and jumped on.

We woke the following morning, feeling fresh and clear-headed. I couldn't remember when I'd last slept so well. And it got better. Bella greeted us with a huge breakfast of sizzling fried eggs and bread and even sausages. I smiled, a proper smile. Real food! Eggs were so scarce. But Bella was a genius at surviving, like Mama, and always found a way.

Bella and Mama started to make plans over breakfast. 'I've spoken to my landlady,' Bella said, 'and told her that you're a friend of mine in need of a place to stay. She has a room you can rent as a subtenant.'

I hung back awkwardly from the conversation. Actually it was because I was embarrassed,

embarrassed to be seen as a girl by someone I knew. I felt like Bella was looking at me differently now. I went back to eating my eggs and sausages, and let Mama and Bella work things out.

'I don't have money for rent, Bella. Don't tenants have to be registered with the police? I'm too afraid to go into town in case anyone in Lwów recognises me! And, anyway, can we trust this friend of yours?'

'It is simple,' said Bella. 'Give, me your papers and I will go.'

Mama looked worried, but handed the papers over. Bella got up immediately and put on dark glasses and a scarf over her head, just like Mama had done when we were in the loft, and headed for the door.

'If I'm not back by five, light a candle for me in church ... and pray,' she said, and slammed the door behind her.

I didn't really understand what Bella meant, why she'd said that. But later that day she returned with our identification papers, with our new registration as a tenant and a booklet of coupons so we could buy bread and potatoes when there were supplies of them.

'But, Bella, how on earth did you get all this?'

'Same way I always do. I stood in the queue and pretended to be you. The clerk asked me where my daughter was and I answered, "In this wet weather, you didn't expect me to bring the child with me, did you?"' She smiled at Mama and gave me a cheeky grin.

Mama gasped. 'Well, I am in awe of you, Bella! Such a risk! If you are such a leading force in the underground, if you conspire against the Germans... well, your face, it will be known by the police, surely? You take great risks for us, my friend. If you'd been recognised? Oh, I hate to think! They'd shoot you on the spot!'

'Well, I wasn't, and they didn't. I cannot sit by and not help, Larissa, you know that. Don't be ridiculous. Everyone needs a guardian angel these days.'

I knew Bella was special. Nobody would ever believe she was half German the way she fought against the Germans now. Mama said that Bella's papa had died fighting for Germany in the Great War. 'Just goes to show, Sasha, not all Germans are bad. Not all are Nazis. Some are humane and selfless. Bella's papa was like that. He just got caught up in a war too, like all of us.' And she sighed and left me to think about that.

Bella was courageous and kind, generous even to the point of going without so that I could have her ration of milk or an extra egg. I loved Bella and we were very lucky to have her help.

But even with Bella's kindness and support, Mama and I still lived in a constant state of fear. If anyone saw us, if they knew us, we'd risk being reported, found out and shot. And now I had such a big part to play in keeping us safe. If I slipped up, forgot I was a girl, both of us would be exposed. Fear constantly plagued me, day and night. Fear of getting caught, fear that we'd die, fear that Bella would also lose her life, fear that the Nazis would win, fear of the annihilation of everything: our present, past and future.

Over the next few weeks as we began to get used to living in our new room, there came through Bella and her network of friends more news of Jews being caught and murdered. News also of the kind Poles who hid them and by doing so lost their lives. And one day, most disturbingly of all, we heard of a place we hadn't heard of before – a place called Auschwitz – another camp so many Jews had been deported to. But now we learnt about what went on there – people spoke of starvation and disease, like all the other camps, and of people being locked in dark airless basement cells where they slowly suffocated. People in the camps had been blinded, maimed and killed by Nazi beatings with sticks or whips.

But then came rumours of something more, of gas chambers, of ovens. I didn't know what to think of these things that Mama and Bella spoke of.

I was beginning to wonder when it would be our turn to face all this. It was only a matter of time. We couldn't keep running forever, always hiding in our room as a gentile mother and daughter. I couldn't keep on pretending to be a girl without people noticing.

And anyway, I knew it was only going to get even more difficult. My voice was breaking. I wanted to look at girls, not be one.

Of course I loved Mama and I knew she was doing this to protect me. But I hated it, and sometimes I'd just lie on the bed and think about what I'd be doing now if there were no war. I'd be going to school, playing football with Sam and Walter, talking to some girls. I looked down at my dress and felt my hair. I felt ashamed. I kept telling myself that I had to be a girl to survive, but none of it felt right – the dress, the walk, how I had to talk, and especially not the shaving I had to do. Mama made me shave my legs as well as my face!

The room we rented was small, but there was a stove where Mama could cook and also a smaller bedroom up some stairs off the main room where we could sleep.

One day, Mama was about to cook some potatoes for us. I was starving and waiting for her to fry them and dish them up for lunch. But then, there was a knock at the door.

'Shhh!' she said urgently. 'Run upstairs! Get into bed. Pretend to be asleep. Go!'

I was terrified. It could be anyone, the SS, the German authorities or, worse, Ukrainians. Ukrainians, we knew, could instantly spot a Jew, while Germans, surprisingly, weren't always so good at picking us.

But we had no choice. We had to open the door. I did as Mama said and ran upstairs, while Mama moved towards the door and slid back the latch.

Her worst fears. Three Ukrainian soldiers!

This time it was too much even for Mama. She panicked and ran out the back door. Maybe she was going to get Bella for help, but I was so afraid of being left by myself, and I prayed the Ukrainians wouldn't come upstairs. But they did. They stormed into the apartment after Mama, found the stairs, and before I knew it they were in the bedroom.

I was wearing my dress, as always, and when the soldiers burst in I just had time to pull the eiderdown up to my chin. I'd grabbed a piece of charcoal and was pretending to be busy drawing on a scrap of paper leant against an old book.

'*Kto tu mieszka?* Who lives here?'

My heartbeat was like a drum in my ears. I had to remember my feminine verbs, keep my answers short. '*Moja matka I ja,*' I answered in a shaky voice. 'There's just Mama and me.'

My hands were trembling under the eiderdown.

Another soldier fired a question at me. '*Jak dlugo tu mieszkacie?* How long have you been living here?'

'*Jak dlugo ja pamietam, barzu dlugo,*' I said, squeezing my sweaty fingers under the warm cover. 'As long as I can remember, a long time.'

'*Jestescie lokatotzy czy sublokatorzy?* Are you tenants or subtenants?'

'*Ja nie wiem.* I don't know.'

I tried to play dumb, my body now drenched in beads of sweat, but I really didn't know the answer to that question. I didn't know the difference between a tenant and a sub anything.

'*Gdzie twoja matka?* Where's your mother?'

'*Ona poszla do pracy.* She went to work.'

'*Gdzie ona pracuje?* Where does she work?'

'*Ja nie wiem. Ja tylko wiem ze ona pracuje dla niemeckiej firmy.* I don't know. I only know she works for a German company.'

Fear surged through my aching bones. And then drops of urine trickled down my legs, wetting my dress under the sheets.

But then the Ukrainian soldiers just looked at each other, nodded their heads and left. An overwhelming sense of panic came over me. Where was Mama? It seemed an eternity before she returned. When she did finally run up the stairs and found me still in the bed she rushed over and hugged me tight. But I was afraid and angry. 'Where did you go? You *left* me when there were soldiers!'

'I ran to Bella for help! I didn't know what else to do!'

'How could you go? How could you leave me here with them?'

Mama's face turned white. Her entire body quivered. I kept yelling at her and repeating the question over and over. And then I was silent, completely exhausted. Mama held me in her arms and cried.

We sat like that for a long time. She tried to hug me tighter, stroke my hair, soothe me and reassure me. But I sat on the bed tight-fisted, clenching my teeth until they hurt, my eyes sore. Mama let me go after a while. She sat opposite me, motionless, on the armchair next to the bed, and whispered her apologies over and over. 'I am sorry, so sorry, my darling! I panicked. I tried to go for help. There was no time. No time to take you.'

I looked away, silent. I sat still, even as night came. And then, finally, I picked up my small stick of charcoal and was going to draw something, anything, just to move and do something, but as I bowed my head over the paper and looked at Mama, I couldn't stop a whimper from breaking out, like a little puppy.

Suddenly, the sobs came. And then tears, so many tears, streaming down my face as I began to shake all over.

Mama got up from her chair and gently took me into her arms, held me close to her chest, and rocked me backwards and forwards on the bed. She began to sing my favourite lullaby. It was called 'Dark Eyes', the one I remembered from when I was little, from the days of Tylda and Binka and cafes and train sets and days of happiness and laughter.

'It's all right, my darling! Sasha, it's all right.' And she continued singing. '*Dark and burning eyes, dark as midnight skies . . .*'

I don't remember how the rest of the night passed or when I fell asleep. All I remember are the words of that Russian lullaby as Mama rocked me to sleep.

The next morning, Bella came to see us. Only then did she learn of the Ukrainian soldiers.

'I couldn't find you!' Mama cried. 'I did a *terrible* thing. I left Sasha, but I couldn't find you. I should never have left him!' She was distraught, shaking her head and wringing her hands. She said over and over to Bella, 'I should not have left him!' Tears flooded down her cheeks.

Bella took her hands and looked closely into her face. 'Larissa, listen to me. You did what you thought was right. You did the only thing you could.' Bella hugged Mama tightly and smiled at me. 'So, I am with you both now,' she said, sounding cheerful and reassuring. 'And you can be absolutely sure of one thing. I will help you survive, with every fibre I have left in my body. Whatever I have to do, whatever it takes. We will all survive. I promise you that.'

Chapter 11
SALA STEPS OUT

Mama and Bella only rarely called me Sasha now and only when they slipped up and forgot. But Sala wasn't the real me – the real me was buried for now, almost forgotten. It was all part of the plan, of course, but the real me didn't want to be Sala. She was me, but not me. I couldn't feel comfortable as a girl. It felt so strange. Foreign, really. It just didn't feel right. And yet, I knew that I had to be one. So now I had a new battle, not just the war I'd been facing for years, but a new war within myself.

For the moment, Mama and I were safe, but after the Ukrainian incident, Bella found us an apartment nearby. We had a hallway, a small living room, one bedroom with two beds, a tiny bathroom and a little corner where two people could sit. It was a cubicle, a tiny sitting space: Mama called it a snug. I loved it because I could sit there with my book for hours and feel tucked away and safe.

It was the end of 1942 now and the weather was getting colder. The war had been going for four years, and I'd almost forgotten how it felt to go to school, to walk in the streets and play with friends. Our news from the outside world was sketchy and unreliable, but Bella and her contacts managed to pass on news, sometimes from the occasional radio broadcast someone had heard.

Mama and I thought about Zayda every day; we couldn't get him out of our heads. We knew murder by the Nazis was a fact of life now. But we still needed to know what was going on. How this news got to us was always unclear and indirect, but we were at least finding out something. There were times, though, when we didn't want to hear it . . .

Like the time we heard about Sonia . . .

We'd only been in our new apartment for about two weeks when information came from a neighbour who'd witnessed things, then passed the story on through friends of friends of friends, all the way to Bella. Zayda's wife Sonia had hidden in a large outdoor rubbish bin the day Zayda had been taken to Belzec. She'd hidden there for days, coming out only to look for something to eat. But, one day, when she was foraging on the street for food, a Nazi soldier stopped and questioned her. He took her to a truck, then to a camp where she was locked alone in a dark cell. The following day, the Nazis made an example of her: she was marched in front of the inmates and shot between the eyes.

And so it went on. The disbelief, the numbness. I cried again that night.

Mama and I also discovered that while we'd been hiding in the barn near Brody, Mama's sister Mania, Stefanie and little Selena had been sheltered by a Polish gentile quite close by. Strange to think they'd been so close by and we hadn't even known they were there.

'Oh, Sasha,' Mama said one evening, forgetting she should've called me Sala. We were sitting in the snug and talking, just to pass the time. 'I know so little. But I do know that Bolek returned from Russia for Mania and Selena. And he was wrongly informed that they were killed. So terrible, and then he surrendered to the Gestapo. I know that Rena's husband Marek never came back for her and that she married Wicek, her former gentile neighbour.'

'Why did Aunty Rena marry her neighbour?' I asked, not knowing why.

'Oh she loved him dearly, Sasha! He helped her a lot, a risky thing – he'd lose his life if the Nazis caught him – but he'd always had a soft spot for Rena.'

'So he helped to hide her?'

'Yes, apparently. She was lucky. He wanted to hide Mania and little Selena as well, she is only three years old, poor darling, but there was no room. Wicek is such a kind man. Look, he managed to get this letter to us too.' Mama took out a small envelope and opened it. She stared at the letter and then looked at me. 'I am not sure I should read it to you...'

'Mama! Don't be stupid, you have to!'

So Mama began to read the letter from my Aunty Mania.

> *My dear Larissa,*
> *I am finding life very difficult hiding with Selena. It is all too much for me. She cries all the time and puts the others hiding here with me at risk. I need you to help us. You are always there when we need you.*
>
> *I don't know how to go on. My life has no meaning without Bolek. I can't seem to cope alone with the child. How long can we go on like hunted animals, only to be murdered by the Nazis?*
>
> *We are still at Marschevsky's, hiding in his cellar. He's a good friend of Marc Krzyinski, Father's old contact. Remember the man who hid you and Sasha for a while? Marschevsky says we have to leave because of Selena's constant crying.*

> *Where are we to go?*
>
> *The others hiding here tell me to get rid of my child! How can I do that? I place my hand over her mouth to hush her crying. You are a mother. What am I to do, Larissa?*
>
> *Your loving sister,*
> *Mania*

Mama had tears in her eyes. 'How can we help? There's nothing I can do!'

'Ask Bella, Mama. Bella always knows.'

'Look, Mania has drawn a map on the back. Perhaps ... if we ask Bella? Yes, you are right. We will ask Bella.'

So the next time we saw Bella, Mama explained Aunty Mania's awful situation. Bella sat silently, read the letter, gave Mama a hug and shook her head. She looked shocked and horrified.

'What are they thinking, Larissa? How can someone even contemplate asking a mother to take the life of her own child? An innocent little girl with a whole life ahead of her!'

Bella sat for a moment, then looked straight at Mama, and briskly clapped her hands on her knees. 'Right! Well now, where are your sister and niece staying?'

Mama didn't quite believe what Bella was asking. 'Bella?'

'You heard me, where are they staying?'

Mama took out the letter and showed Bella the map that Mania had included.

'Well, there we are!' said Bella in her matter-of-fact way. 'This is good. We can find them.'

'But how will that help?'

'Leave it with me, Larissa.' And that was the end of that conversation with Bella.

One week later we learnt what Bella had done. She'd paid Marschevsky another 1000 *zlotys* to keep Mania and her family safe. Bella knew the value of a bribe.

Another week later Bella was back in our apartment, hoping to help more.

'Now, your other sisters, Larissa? Can we do anything for them?' she asked.

'Well, I don't know. My sister Rena is safe with Wicek, I hope. And Binka stayed in Brody and is safe for now. At least that's what I heard,' Mama explained.

'If you hear anything, anything we can do, you let me know, Larissa.'

And then one day, Mama did hear something. Wicek wrote out of the blue to tell Mama he was coming to see her about a pressing matter.

'What pressing matter?' I asked.

'Never you mind, Sasha, I mean, Sala . . . We'll find out when he arrives.'

A few days later Wicek knocked on our door, and both Mama and I were so pleased to see his friendly, familiar face. Except, of course, Wicek looked at me and paused.

'I didn't know you had a young girl with you, Larissa. And where is Sasha?'

Mama laughed and hugged him tightly. 'Oh Wicek! The things I have to do to keep us safe. This *is* Sasha. He only looks like a girl – so he won't be discovered as a Jewish boy!'

'I am astounded. Larissa, what a clever idea!'

Why everyone thought it was so clever I had no idea. Wicek wouldn't think it was clever if he had to dress up as a girl.

Mama and Wicek talked for a long time that day. They talked about my aunts, about the war, about people I didn't know. Then Wicek stopped and looked very serious. We braced ourselves for more bad news.

'Larissa, my cousin Ella . . . she needs help. I have no one else I can ask.'

'Of course we'll help, Wicek. What is wrong?'

'Ella . . . she's pregnant. But she can't have a baby now, not in this war. To bring a child into this world, surrounded by death and fear! She needs help.'

'I see,' said Mama.

'She wants an abortion. But she is ashamed, embarrassed! She doesn't know where to go.'

I could see Mama was wondering how on earth she could do anything at all. 'Well, I will inquire for you, Wicek, but –'

'She isn't Jewish!' Wicek added. 'She looks almost Aryan – blue eyes and blondish hair. That will make it easier, Larissa.'

'Yes, yes, of course. All right, Wicek. Leave this with me. Bella will know about a doctor. Ella and Rena could stay somewhere near here. Between us all we'll get Ella out of this mess.'

'Thank you, my dear Larissa! I will hear from you then.' Wicek kissed Mama on the cheek, nodded towards me with a smile and left.

I didn't hear anything more about babies or Ella after that. All I knew was that Mama had been true to her word – she'd found a way to help Ella. And two weeks later Mama and I received another unexpected visitor.

'Binka!' exclaimed Mama when she opened the door one morning. 'Binka, oh, Binka! You are here?'

'Yes, here I am, sister!'

'But... how on earth did you get here?' She hugged her sister and hurried her quickly inside.

'A German soldier fancied me. Gave me a ride.'

'*German!*'

'It's all right, Larissa. He has no idea I'm Jewish.'

'No *idea*? Binka! He's German! He knows where you are. If he even so much as *suspects* . . .'

'Don't worry, I –'

'*Worry?* Didn't he ask to see your papers?'

'No, of course not! All he's interested in are my legs.' She laughed.

'*Binka!*'

'Larissa, it's fine.'

'This isn't funny, Binka! This is far too dangerous, accepting lifts from Germans. He could trace you here, to us . . .'

'Relax, for God's sake, Larissa. I have blonde hair and blue eyes and look nothing like a Jew. I told him I was Catholic.'

'Oh, did you?'

'Anyway, I'm here now.'

'Yes, well . . . I am so happy that you are here, of course I am, but don't go taking stupid risks. You will get us all killed.'

'And where is Sasha? Is he awake?' asked Binka, changing the subject.

'He's having a nap.'

'No, I'm here,' I said, coming out from the bedroom at last.

When Binka saw me her face fell into the weirdest look of disbelief I'd ever seen.

'Sasha?'

'Yes, it's me, Aunty Binka. Really!'

Binka looked at Mama, then back at me.

'We'll explain...' began Mama.

'Why on earth do you have such long hair?' And then a sudden look of realisation came over her face. 'And that's my dress. You're wearing my *dress*!'

I went bright red.

'Binka, listen...' Mama said. 'We had to find a way of saving Sasha from being discovered as a Jewish boy.'

'So you grew his hair and let him wear my *dress*?'

'Well... yes.'

'And the high-pitched voice?' Binka still looked overwhelmingly shocked.

'Well, I taught him to talk like a girl.'

'A girl?'

'Yes, and he's done a wonderful job, Binka! And his voice hasn't really broken yet. Not completely. And he's learnt to give himself a clean shave...'

Binka didn't say anything for ages. She just stood there in this awkward, painful silence. Until at last she said, very quietly to Mama, 'Larissa, have you gone *mad*?'

At last, I thought. Someone who understands.

'Binka, we ran out of options! It's Sasha's last hope of survival. He is Sala now.'

Binka still looked completely bewildered. Mama made her sit down at our dining table.

'I will explain the whole story, Binka,' Mama said. I sat with them, silently listening, but inside all I wanted to do was give Aunty Binka a big hug and tell her that I was still Sasha, her nephew, and that nothing had really changed at all.

When Mama finally finished telling Binka how she'd got our papers, and all the details of teaching me to become a girl, Binka put her arm around me and kissed me on the cheek. 'Sasha, my brave boy! You are safe! That is all that matters.'

That night, Mama and Binka sat on the edge of my bed and tucked me in. They sang me my favourite Russian lullaby, 'Dark Eyes', again.

Dark and burning eyes. Dark as midnight skies
Full of passion flame, full of lovely game.

I must have fallen asleep eventually. I remember thinking, this is like the happy times, and I thought of the cafes of Lwów, and of my friends Sam and Walter and wondered if they were in bed asleep too.

I woke the next day and remembered at once that Binka my darling aunt was back with us once more.

Chapter 12
THE REAL GIRLS IN MY LIFE

The best part about Binka being back was that now I had someone to talk to. Talking to Mama wasn't the same as talking to Binka. I could tell Binka things I wouldn't ever tell Mama.

One morning Binka and I were sitting together in the snug while Mama had gone to buy food. 'Well, Sasha, I suppose I have to call you Sala too!' Binka smiled, but I didn't feel like smiling back.

'Don't worry, you won't have to do this forever.'

'But I hate pretending all the time! Mama has no idea how hard it is.'

'I'm sure she does. She knows.'

'And I hate this stupid dress!'

'My dress.'

'Well... yes, but you're a girl. You're meant to wear a dress. I'm not.'

'I know, Sasha... Sala.'

'And I have to keep shaving, and my voice is starting to get deeper too – it's been doing that for ages, going up and down. It's not so easy any more.'

'It's a lot to ask of anyone, but a young boy...'

'I'm scared. If my voice breaks at the wrong moment I'll be discovered. If I slip up on even one tiny thing. And thinking of the grammar all the time. I hate grammar. I hate this war!'

'We must all just try to do our best to survive. And soon, I pray, we will be free.'

'Binka?'

'Yes?'

'I think about girls now. I don't want to *be* one.'

'You don't need to worry,' Binka said reassuringly. 'After the war you'll be so handsome that all the girls will love you.'

'I won't ever tell them I used to wear a dress.'

'No, perhaps not,' she said, and she laughed. 'Just concentrate on not being discovered for now. I know it is hard and it might feel as though you are being pulled apart inside, but it is a tug of war that will keep you safe.' Aunty Binka put her arm around me and we sat there silently until Mama came in the door.

By the end of that week, there was another unexpected family reunion. I was beginning to feel hopeful – our family was coming together again.

Mama heard a knock on our door, hesitated to open it as we always did, and then found two strangers standing there. Two women, one holding a letter, the other holding the hand of a little girl. Mama stood there, silent, until one of the women said, 'This is Selena,' and passed Mama the letter. They pushed the little girl forward and left.

Mama looked at the child in complete shock. Selena? She was so little. And she just stared up at Mama, and then at me and Binka standing over by the hall door. We hadn't seen Selena for years. She was just a baby when we last saw her.

Mama shook herself into action and gently led Selena into our apartment. She stared at Binka in disbelief, and opened the letter.

'Well, read it out, Larissa, for God's sake. We need to know what's going on too.'

So Mama began to read.

Dear Larissa,
Forgive me for doing this, but as none of your letters have reached me, I feel I have no choice. The others hiding with me are frightened they will be discovered with Selena's constant cries. They begged me to do something. My child is a good girl and I am sure you will ensure her safety. I just can't keep her here any longer.
Mania

'That's it?' said Binka.

'Yes, that's it!' said Mama.

Selena started to whimper, so Binka took her in her arms and sat with her on our sofa. The little girl looked terrified. Worse than terrified. She looked... vacant somehow. But the most terrible thing of all was what she was saying.

'Larissa...' said Binka. 'Listen to her!'

Selena was saying something over and over, almost like chanting.

'What's she saying?' said Mama. 'I can't make it out.'

Selena, stared back at Mama, clearly very frightened.

'Selena, darling,' Mama said, 'tell us what you want, dear. What is it?'

And then suddenly we all grasped the words at once, what Selena was saying in her tiny little voice.

Over and over she repeated the same words, and they sent a chill down my spine.

'Oh, dear God!' said Binka.

Selena began again. '*Ssh, ssh!* Be quiet!' she said in that little girl voice. 'Ssh, ssh! Or the Germans will *shoot* you. Be quiet! *Be quiet!*'

'The poor, poor creature!' Mama cried. 'Binka, whatever are we to do?'

'*Ssh, ssh!* Be quiet. Be *quiet!*' Selena repeated. Over and over and over.

I didn't want to hear any more. I couldn't bear the sound.

I ran to my room and lay on my bed, tears beginning to form in my eyes.

Mama and Binka made a big fuss over Selena. They fed her, kissed her and cuddled her constantly. They sang songs to her, even my special song 'Dark Eyes'. I gritted my teeth when I heard them singing that. Now it was Selena who was wrapped in warm blankets, and sung to – anything to stop her from chanting those dreadful words.

'It's going to be a tight squeeze in here now, with Binka sleeping with me and Selena at the other end of Sala's bed,' Mama said.

As if the song wasn't enough. Now I had to share my bed with her.

Selena was very quiet for the first few weeks. She hardly spoke except to repeat her disturbing chant. 'Ssh, ssh, the Germans will *shoot* you!'

I tried asking her questions, but she never responded. I tried reading to her, but I don't think she listened. After a few days I gave up trying to communicate with words. It wasn't going to work. So I began to chase her instead, which sounds weird, but I thought if she didn't want to talk then she might just like to play. So I chased her, teasingly, all around our small apartment. At first she just watched, and I felt a bit stupid just running around by myself, but eventually she got up and then she started to follow me and try and find where I'd gone. That never took long because there were only about three different places I could hide anyway. Then one day she suddenly let out a nervous little giggle and began to join in.

'Sala, you are a genius!' Mama said. 'Talking to her was never going to work. But a game.'

In front of Selena I always pretended faithfully to be a girl. Mama and Binka thought this was best for now, because Selena was so young she might easily blurt something out in front of someone who could betray us. Selena had to believe that I was a real girl.

At least I had someone to play with now. And I started to watch how Selena did things too, how she acted like a girl naturally, her mannerisms, her slightly irritating girly shyness, and I tried to imitate all this in front of the mirror when no one was watching. I tried to smile like she smiled. I tried swishing my head from left to right like she did, and I even learnt how to curtsey in my dress. It was a bit like being in a play where I had to act the part of a girl, and I began to enjoy practising at being completely convincing. I was fascinated by Selena now, how I could play with her without using words at all. And very soon she stopped chanting her words about the

Germans altogether. She still didn't say much, but at least she'd stopped saying, 'Ssh, ssh, the Germans will shoot you.'

But Mama didn't know how long we could go on caring for Selena. 'It is so hard! The child wants her mother. She just cries and cries for her. It's not right.'

'Whenever you don't know what to do you ask Bella, Mama,' I suggested.

'Yes, of course. Bella.' And that's exactly what Mama did.

'What about Rena and Wicek?' Bella asked. 'They could take the child.'

Bella's suggestion made perfect sense. Rena had more space than us. But I'd become so used to having Selena around over the last few months that I was sad to think of her going. 'Of course you are, Sala!' Mama said. 'You are blood, family, and you have the war in common. Of course you will miss her, but I have you to think of too. I am sure Selena will be happy with Rena.'

So arrangements were made. Bella helped Mama get an apartment in our building, especially for Rena, Wicek and Selena. And Mama was overjoyed to have her two sisters close by again.

But Mama's mind was far from settled. At night I could hear her tossing and turning in her bed, and

I knew she was troubled by nightmares. I was too, ever since we learnt Zayda had died. But one night I heard her let out a scream. I sat bolt upright in my bed and waited.

Mama got up, went into the living room and turned on a lamp. I followed to see if she was all right. She was sitting on the sofa, her nightgown soaked with sweat.

'It's all right, Sala. Just a bad dream, that's all.'

'I have bad dreams too,' I said.

'Yes, of course you do. We all do, I am sure.'

'What was your dream about, Mama?'

'About Zayda. I often dream about Zayda.'

'Me too.'

'He was calling me. I could see his face . . .' Mama's eyes were full of tears, but she seemed to gather strength then and said firmly, 'Enough of this. I will have a bath. Go back to bed. You need your sleep.'

I knew why Mama had wanted a bath. When I woke up, clammy and sweaty from a bad dream, I wanted to get rid of that feeling of grime and sweat too. Once, after a bad nightmare about Zayda, I'd got into the bath and suddenly imagined the bath filling not with water but with blood, Zayda's blood seeping out of him as he lay dying. I shuddered. I hoped Mama didn't imagine the same. That night I couldn't shake off a terrible sense of being in grave danger.

By now many Jews around us had gone into permanent hiding. About twenty-four were hiding in the bunker of a farm not far from us.

'You know some of them, Larissa,' Binka said. 'The farm is owned by the Kalwinski family. The lawyer next to Lansberg. In Sykstuska Street. The one who has a doctorate in law.'

Mama stared at Binka blankly.

'You know, Larissa. The one who converted his home into an office. And Edmund Kessler and his wife, Fryderyka, are hiding at the farm too. Those kind Poles – risking their lives to hide so many. They are feeding them, washing their clothing. They are astonishingly good people!'

The Kalwinski farm was about two and a half kilometres from the centre of Lwów. They grew all their own food – strawberries, cabbages, rye and wheat. A stable sheltered their horses, cows and pigs, and they also had turkeys and hens. So the Kalwinskis shared whatever they had with the Jewish refugees: they did what they thought was right.

Mama, Binka and I still had our apartment, but the bombings in Lwów had started again and, during the bombing raids, we sheltered in the basement of our apartment building along with the other tenants.

I hated going down there. The cellars were dark and stifling, crowded with people, and often we didn't know how long we'd have to stay down there. One day, I found myself separated from Mama and Binka as we'd run quickly to the cellar amongst the crowd of other residents. I don't know how it happened, but I lost sight of Mama and Binka before we even got to the cellar. I'd been playing in the hallway with some of the other children in the building, including a slightly older boy called Berkowitz. He'd often tease me, so I tried to avoid him if I could. But now, in the confusion and rush to the shelter, I found myself crouched in a corner, and Berkowitz was beside me.

After some minutes, I was suddenly aware of Berkowitz's hand on my neck. He was stroking my hair! I said nothing, but my heart was beating hard in my chest, and I didn't know what to do. I'd have to push through an enormous amount of people to get away from him. So I tried to shrug him off, but then, to my absolute horror, Berkowitz whispered, 'Sssh!' and bent his head to my neck and kissed it.

I couldn't believe it! I was too afraid to draw attention to myself. What would a real girl do in this situation? I turned my head away. Berkowitz seemed to get the message, but then after only a few minutes I felt a hand against my leg. Berkowitz had managed to get his hand under my dress and was moving it slowly up my thigh.

This was truly terrifying now. I'd be discovered! Berkowitz would find out I was a boy. I leapt up and, ignoring the complaints of people whose feet I'd trodden on, I ran from the cellar as fast as I could and sheltered in a doorway until the rest of the bombing stopped.

When I finally got back to our apartment, Mama wasn't there.

'She was out of her mind with worry, Sala!' Binka said, frantically clutching my arm. 'We couldn't find you!'

'I had to get away! I couldn't breathe with all those people in the cellar.'

'But you know it's not safe outside!'

Binka was about to go and search the streets for Mama when the front door burst open and Mama stormed in, her face flushed and distraught. 'Sala! What happened? Where *were* you?'

But I was angry by now, angry at the whole situation. 'I've had enough of being a girl!' I shouted. 'I can't stand this any more!' And I began to undo the buttons of my dress.

'Sala?' Mama started to come and hug me, but I didn't want to be hugged. I didn't want to be touched at all. I felt humiliated. I went into the bedroom and slammed the door. No, I would never tell Mama what had happened. She'd put me in this situation, this whole masquerade. It was her fault I'd been touched like that by another boy.

Mama and Binka left me alone that night. I lay there thinking about how long I was going to have to carry on this charade, behaving like a girl. One mistake would mean the end of my life. And I really wanted to live. I wanted to play football again with other boys out in the open air. I wanted to flirt with girls. Even now I thought about getting to know their bodies and getting to know how they thought and what they liked, not just how they acted and talked.

I never did tell Mama about that night in the cellar.

Not long after the cellar incident, Mama heard on the grapevine that Mania was still safe, hiding in a cellar on the outskirts of Brody. But others were not so lucky. She heard some distressing news of a close friend called Avram. He'd been in the Janowska camp in Lwów, taken there from the ghetto and forced to perform carpentry and metalwork. It was unsanitary, where they housed all those enforced workers, and they were poorly fed. After a while Avram was hanged for working too slowly.

We heard about others too – relatives of friends, old acquaintances, neighbours – who'd been shot, or flogged or stabbed to death at Janowska. Many had already died from disease. We heard talk that the site became a transit camp for Jews from the villages and towns nearby: those fit enough to work were selected and the unfit were sent on to Belzec.

Now late in 1942, the Janowska camp had turned into an extermination centre. They were sending thousands of Jews to their deaths.

Chapter 13
EVA

My life had become chaotic again, just when I thought our apartment would be a haven from the worst of the war.

It wasn't the war outside now – it was the war inside that was hard to cope with. The problem, Mama said, was that each sister thought they knew what was best for Selena.

'Well, I don't know, really I don't, Sala. Rena wants it this way, and Binka wants it that way, and little Selena is caught in the middle. Of course everyone thinks they're right! And everyone has a different opinion on how to bring her up.'

Some days it was quite funny, listening to them all. 'Selena, don't eat with your fingers,' Mama would say. 'It's not good manners.'

'Oh, leave the girl alone, Larissa!' Rena would say. 'She's only a child!'

And then right on queue Binka would come in singing and grab Selena around the waist and waltz around the apartment with her, making her giggle as they weaved between the furniture.

'Binka!' Mama said, 'What d'you think you're doing? It's the child's dinnertime.'

They started to argue again then, about who was right and who knew best. And then they started to shout at each other. I just couldn't figure Mama and her sisters out sometimes. I caught Selena's eye and nodded for her to come and play instead. Mama, Binka and Rena didn't even notice because Binka had put Selena down again at the table and they were all so busy arguing that Selena and I quietly disappeared to my bedroom and looked at books instead.

All this stuff with Selena and my aunts just made me worry about myself again, struggling to pretend to be a girl. Binka tried to help me understand what it was like being a girl. She even showed me how to put on make-up one day. I'd gone to use the bathroom, but Binka was already there.

'Come in, Sala. I won't be long. I am just putting on mascara.'

'What?'

'Mascara. Girls do it to lengthen their eyelashes. See? And now I'm drawing my eyebrows with a pencil, to make my eyes stand out more. And then . . .'

I thought this was ridiculous. There was no way I was going to start wearing make-up.

'I start on the lips.' Binka puckered her lips and

painted some bright-red lipstick onto them. 'See how lovely they look!' She smiled.

I didn't know what to say. If she came anywhere near me with that stuff I'd run a mile.

'Oh, I forgot the rouge!' she said, and grabbed a compact from her handbag. She dabbed red powder on her cheeks. I had no idea why that was necessary at all.

'But Binka, it's the war and we're hiding. No one cares if you have make-up on or not.'

'Well, there might be a war,' Binka said, suddenly sounding annoyed, 'but I am damned if I'm going to let the Nazis stop me from looking good.'

I still didn't get it. Going through that paint ritual would be hideous. The dress and the hair were bad enough.

'Besides,' Binka went on, 'your mama's birthday is coming up and I'm going to look nice for that if it kills me. Oh, I hope we can get her some flowers or something! Wouldn't that be wonderful?'

I could never really escape from Mama and my aunts and all this girl stuff. I loved them and wanted them to be around, but sometimes they got under my skin. And Mama was always Mama, I guess, and she always meant well, but she was strong-willed and determined, and I knew her sisters sometimes thought she always got her own way. Maybe that's why we'd survived so long, when many others around us hadn't.

Really I just wanted someone my age to be with, but there were only a few other gentile children in our apartment block. I tried to make friends but it was difficult. Three of them were the daughters of our landlady Mrs Polonski: Gisela the eldest, then Eva and Gerda. Eva was the same age as me and she liked some of the same things. I managed to teach her how to play chess, using an old chess set Mrs Polonski had. There was no board so Eva and I had to draw one up on a piece of old cardboard, but chess was something that reminded me of the real me – Sasha. And that was great.

Except it isn't easy being friends with a girl when you are pretending to be a girl. And the better friends we became the worse it got.

One day when we were playing together, Eva suddenly stopped what she was doing and looked straight at my chest. 'Sala, why is your chest so *flat*? My bosoms are already quite full,' she said proudly, showing off a bit. 'Why haven't yours grown yet?'

I was speechless. I turned red. I had no idea how to answer. When were girls' bosoms supposed to get bigger? I had to think quickly, and remembered the line Mama sometimes used. 'Well, I don't know . . . maybe I'm a late developer?'

Eva frowned and seemed to lose interest.

I tried to steer the conversation onto other things. I told Mama about it later that day. 'And what did you say, Sala?'

'I didn't know what to say! I just laughed it off. But I'll have to do something to be more girly. She seems a bit suspicious now . . . about who I am.'

Mama began to look worried. 'Well, what do you think will work?'

'I have no idea, Mama.'

Mama thought some more. 'Girls sometimes have baths together. Eva does that with her sisters. To save soap. She asked me if you wanted to stay and share a bath with them once. Perhaps if you did that . . .'

'But how could I do *that*?'

'We'll work out a way. If *I* run a bath, here, in our apartment, and you get in before she comes over?'

I stared at Mama. I could see what she was thinking.

'I'll run the bath so that it's very full. Your whole body would be covered. And I'll use lots of soap so there are lots of bubbles. Don't worry, Eva won't see a thing.'

I wasn't convinced. It was just another one of Mama's harebrained schemes. 'But what if she wants to hop in with me?' I was horrified.

'She can! The water will be so soapy and bubbly and

your body totally covered. Just tuck all your . . . bits in and she won't see a thing! The bathroom door can stay open and I'll be in the next room if you need me. I'm sure it will work.'

I wish I'd never mentioned Eva and her suspicions now. But Mama was right, again. I had no choice. Eva must be convinced, beyond any doubt. If she said anything to anyone, if she voiced any doubt at all, it could lead to unthinkable consequences.

That week we chose a day when Eva would be over at our apartment. I'd spent extra time making sure I'd shaved in all the right places, making sure my face was free of even the tiniest hairs. I used Mama's eyebrow tweezers as well as a shaver and discovered that tweezers hurt like hell.

Mama was preparing dinner when Eva came over. Mama went quickly into the bathroom as planned and began to fill the bath with water, nearly to the top, adding as much soap as she could. Eva and I went into my bedroom to look at books until Mama poked her head around the door.

'Eva, come into the kitchen and talk to me for a moment. Sala is about to have her bath. Go on, Sala, in you get, before the water gets cold.'

I smiled at Eva and ran into the bathroom. I thought I was pretty convincing with my walking now. I quickly undressed behind the bathroom door and immediately lowered myself into the hot, soapy water. I made sure there were lots of bubbles over my chest so she wouldn't see how flat it was. And the bath was so full it nearly overflowed.

I heard Mama begin a long conversation with Eva, all about her mother and sisters, how they were, what they were cooking, how they were managing with the food shortages. Eva was a polite girl and answered all of Mama's questions and seemed to be enjoying the chat. From the bath I could hear everything they said. For a moment I imagined Eva naked, getting into the bath with me. I thought about seeing her totally nude, like a painter's model. But I had to stop thinking like this! I was meant to be a girl! The moment had come. I had to call her in.

'Eva, come and talk to me! I'm in the bath still.'

I had to admit that Eva was attractive. She had thick reddish-blonde hair braided into a long plait, a beautiful turned-up nose, and large green eyes. Her body was... curvy, I suppose, and I couldn't help noticing it. I wondered what Mama would think if she knew what I was actually thinking.

Eva came into the bathroom, and to my horror she shut the door behind her. But I needed the door open! So I could hear Mama and she could hear me!

Eva smiled. 'Oooh, a bubble bath!' And then

things got . . . difficult. She started unbuttoning her blouse. I glanced away, pretending to be interested in a chipped tile instead. How stupid was that! Then Eva slipped off her skirt and dropped her underpants onto the floor. She climbed into the foamy water, splashing some over the edge, and sat smiling opposite me. I gathered up an armful of bubbles and pressed them to my chest.

I really really wanted that bathroom door open. If Mama didn't know the door was closed she wouldn't know I couldn't call out to her. How would she know what was happening in here?

Fortunately Mama came to check. The handle of the bathroom door turned slowly and Mama nudged the door ajar so she could see me without Eva noticing. Mama could see that I was totally covered in bubbles in all the right places, and I was sitting with my knees up to my chest. There was no way Eva could see that I wasn't a girl.

But after only a few minutes, she couldn't stand the tension any longer. She cut the bath session short. 'Eva, darling, our dinner is ready and it's probably time for yours too. Out of the bath now. Your mama will be looking for you!'

I took a deep breath of relief, and another when I saw Eva get out of the bath and dry herself with a towel. She dressed quickly and had her back to me for most of the time, but I wished for a moment that I could touch her soft skin, and when she suddenly turned around to say something to me I noticed for a split second the reddish-brown hair between her legs. I'd no idea what Eva said to me then: I couldn't concentrate on anything. It was the first time I'd ever seen a girl's private parts. I glanced away and hoped that Eva hadn't seen that I was blushing.

But she hadn't seemed to notice anything. She said goodbye cheerily and headed for the front door. I climbed out of the bath, dried myself and then all I remember was walking to my bedroom. I felt dizzy, I remember that much. And then everything went black.

The next thing I knew I was lying on the carpet in the hall and Mama was leaning over me.

'Sala? What on earth's happened?' She seemed to gather me up in her arms, and I'm not sure how she did it but somehow she managed to carry me or drag me to my bed. 'Sala! Can you hear me? Oh God, oh God, what *is* the matter?' She covered me with my quilt. I was shivering, but I opened my eyes and took a few moments to work out where I was and who I was looking at.

'Where am I?'

'You're with me, Sala! You've just had a bath. Eva was here, remember? You're home, safe and sound.' She stroked my head and wrapped the quilt around me.

'I thought I was asleep.' I began to cry because I'd woken up but couldn't work out what was real and what wasn't. I felt dizzy. 'I don't know who I am! I was a girl! But then I saw a girl! With no clothes on. But I'm not a girl, am I?' I tried to catch my breath. 'I *am* a boy! I'm a boy!'

Mama began to cry then. 'Oh Sala! Your face is *white*. All this deception, it's just no good for you.' She looked at me as though she thought I was going mad. 'It's all right. Truly it is! Soon we will be free. You'll be yourself again. The war will end and . . .'

Mama kept talking to me and hugging the quilt around me. She said something about Eva and something about everything being all right. She kept repeating that bit, over and over. 'The truth that you are really a boy . . . to others this would mean your death. And I *will* not risk that. *Never!*' And then she calmed herself. 'But, of course, this is silly . . . all you need is rest, not more of me talking. I will call Bella. She will know what to do.'

I slept for the rest of that evening and into the night. In the morning Mama came in to tell me that Bella had once again arranged a doctor. He'd be here soon, and that I was to rest. I dozed off and on, until I heard the doorbell ring.

'Sala, darling, there is a nice doctor here to see you. His name is Dr Sokoloski. He is Polish, a friend of Bella's.' She smiled at me, but she looked nervous. She tucked the quilt around me and a few minutes later she led the doctor into my bedroom.

He looked at me and smiled. 'So this is your daughter? Hello, Sala, my dear. What seems to be the problem?'

I had no idea what I should say, but Mama quickly stepped. 'Sash...ah...Sala...she was having a bath yesterday evening, just before dinner, and when she got out she fainted, here, in the hall.'

'Well, she does look a little on the pale side. Very pale. Does she get enough fresh air?' I was glad he seemed to be talking to Mama more than to me.

'Well, as much as she can.'

'Has she started her period yet?'

This was too much even for Mama then. She simply burst into tears.

'My goodness, Mrs Fein! What on earth is the matter? It's just a simple question!'

'But she is not a she!'

The doctor looked horrified. 'I am sure I don't know what you mean, Mrs Fein.'

And then Mama explained everything, the entire truth about me living as a girl for the past year and a bit. The doctor turned white. He remained silent.

'But I beg of you, you must say nothing! Please . . . just tell me he is all right. Tell me what I should do. But promise me that you will keep our secret!'

But we didn't need to be afraid. The doctor was a good man. We should have known Bella would not have entrusted us to someone who would betray us. The doctor took Mama's hand. 'My dear woman, calm yourself. Of course I will say nothing. Let me examine your son. Let me see what I can do.'

So the doctor simply took my temperature, looked at my eyes and ears and listened to my chest, and prescribed some sort of calming drug for me to steady my nerves. I'd had enough shocks – but I wasn't likely to be shocked by having to pretend to be female in front of a naked girl twice in one week.

Early next morning I woke up hungry. I was feeling much better, and if Mama had to go out to shop for food then I'd be fine by myself for a while. I really needed some food by now. I was starving. Besides, my aunts weren't far off and I could always get one of them to stay with me while she was out. So Mama agreed and left to buy more groceries where she could – our supplies were running low with extra people in the apartment now. But when Mama came home, only about an hour later, she was distressed and almost in tears.

'What is it now, Mama? Were there Germans? Ukrainians?

'No, Sala. Well, not exactly. No soldiers. I met a young woman called Akalena. But, yes, she is Ukrainian, and I used to work with her before the war.'

'So did she talk to you?'

'Yes, she called out to me. I tried to hide but there was nowhere to run. I was so frightened!'

'Why?'

'Well, I thought she'd give me away, so I asked her, "How much to keep quiet?" But she said she didn't want any money. She said she saw me on the tram, but the tram was marked *Nur Für Deutsche*. Germans Only. Oh, Sala, I didn't see! I had no idea. Akalena was trying to warn me, save me from making a terrible mistake.'

'Well, she was trying to help then.'

'Yes, and she gave me her address – another contact if we need help. How kind! She said she remembered how well I'd treated her when she was a cleaning lady at the office. I'd given her time off because her son was ill. I remember now . . .' Mama said softly.

I didn't understand why Mama had been so upset by the encounter with Akalena. She'd been helpful, not dangerous. Maybe it was because Mama always had to risk herself outside the apartment that she was so frightened and nervous all the time. But there wasn't much I could do to help her because I wasn't allowed outside. I was fourteen now; I should've been more of a help to Mama, been the man of the house, looking after her instead. But I couldn't. Not as a girl. Not as a boy who'd die if he were discovered.

But then I remembered suddenly what Binka had said about Mama and her birthday. I could plan a surprise for her! Brilliant idea! I could use some small change Mama had left for me in case of emergencies. It was worth the risk.

While Mama was out shopping for vegetables that week, I quietly slipped out of the apartment.

Normally, I didn't ever go outside and if I did it was after dark and only with Mama. But I knew where to go and what I had to do. As long as I was careful . . .

I kept to the streets I knew, stayed in the shadows and to the sides of the buildings. I didn't look at anyone and walked quickly so I looked busy and as though I knew exactly where I was going. It didn't take me long to get to the market, and the flower stall was easy to spot with all its colourful, beautiful bunches of flowers. I tried to look a bit shy and pointed to a small bunch of white and purple flowers, and the woman behind the stall just smiled and took my change. Thank goodness I had enough. I took the flowers and turned to go home. Out of the corner of my eye, I spotted Jurek, my former Ukrainian neighbour, a boy I used to play with.

And then suddenly there was someone standing right next to me. And a voice. A German voice. I found out what they were saying later.

'*Einige blumen für ihre mutter, ya?*' Some flowers for your mother?

I looked up. A German soldier. SS.

'*Sehr hübsch!*' Very pretty!

I was terrified. I had no idea what he was saying. I smiled as naturally as I could, turned and ran home. I prayed and prayed he wouldn't follow. He didn't.

But someone else did.

When I returned, Mama was already home and she was very angry. 'Where on earth were you? I was just about to call Bella – I was so afraid!'

'Happy birthday, Mama!' I said proudly as I presented her with the white and purple flowers from behind my back. I kissed her and hugged her tightly.

Mama forgot about being angry and looked as though she would cry.

'Oh, Sala! Flowers! For my birthday! It's been such a long time since anyone . . . oh, they are beautiful!'

'I wanted you to feel special today.'

'Come and sit down. I will find a vase. But you must tell me, did anyone see you?'

'I went to the market in the centre of town. There was a boy I noticed . . .' I didn't mention the SS officer.

'But who?'

'I think it was Jurek, that Ukrainian boy who used to live next door.'

'Did he follow you?'

'Yes, a little way. I turned as many corners as I could and ran faster and eventually lost him. I think it is all right, Mama.'

'You shouldn't have gone out. It was a big risk for a bunch of flowers.'

I was silent for a minute, then lifted my chin up to look at Mama. 'But it's your birthday, and I am fine.'

'Come here and let me hug you,' Mama said softly, looking at me with tears in her eyes once more.

Mama made potato cakes again for dinner that night. That was all she could make. But we didn't care. Her birthday flowers were in a vase in front of us, and for once I felt very happy.

Just before bedtime, Mama and I went over to the balcony and looked outside. The sky was a soft grey colour and I could see clouds that looked like fluffed-up cushions. Another cloud streaked in white and grey caught my attention. I kept staring at it until my eyes wandered over to the other side of the sky where I could see beautiful shades of grey and pink. Sometimes it amazed me that there was still such beauty in our world, which was so torn apart by the war.

I looked at Mama and thought about our earlier life in Lwów. All we'd ever wanted to do was live quietly, love our family and be loved in return. But now two people in our lives who were so dear to us were gone – Zayda and Bubbe. And then I thought of my papa, dying so early. Now, the war had taken her father and brother too. But she still had her sisters – and me.

Mama put her arm around me and led me inside away from the cool night air. 'Come on, Sala. You mean everything to me, you know that. All my hopes and dreams are for you now. All my present and my future. My whole world. I must always keep you safe!'

Chapter 14
ZEGOTA

Early one morning, I woke with a start. Mama was still lying beside me, and she grabbed my shoulder and whispered suddenly in my ear.

'Sssh!' she said in a voice I could barely hear. 'There was someone screaming! From the apartment opposite. It must have been Cilla.'

Cilla was Mrs Polonski, our landlady. I glanced over at Mama who put a finger to her lips.

Suddenly we heard a sound that chilled us to the bone, the unmistakable sound of heavy boots, German boots, clunking up the stairs. Then loud German voices echoing through the thin walls of our apartment building.

My heart was pounding furiously. A voice demanded, *'Wo sind die Juden?'*

Oh God, oh God, oh God, I thought. This was finally our end. I knew that *Juden* meant Jews. They were looking for Jews.

'Ich weiß nicht, was du redest!' We could hear Mrs Polonski answer.

'Sie wissen sehr gut, sie hure.' The German had

answered. Loud voices. Yelling and thumping and slamming doors.

Then came another scream. I jumped out of bed then. 'No! Sala!' Mama glared at me, but I ran out into the hall to look through the peephole in our front door.

I could see Mrs Polonski's door from across the corridor. It was open and a Nazi soldier and a Ukrainian policeman were standing there. And then I watched as something dreadful happened, so dreadful I can almost see it, still, today. The Nazi grabbed Mrs Polonski, threw her to the ground, and kicked her viciously in the stomach.

'*Bitte aufhören! Bitte aufhören!* She begged them to stop, and I saw her clutching at the rug on the floor, struggling to regain her feet.

I wanted to run and help. I wanted to kill those Nazis right there and then. I didn't care what they did to me. But there was Mama... I had to think of Mama...

I ran back to our bedroom and I didn't need to tell her what I'd seen. She'd heard enough. 'Get back into bed!' she hissed. 'Pretend you are asleep!'

It was barely a minute later when we heard the soldiers beat on our own front door. They began to force it open. The blood chilled in my veins. I don't know how Mama remained so calm, but she quietly got out of bed, gestured quickly at me to stay put, and moved slowly towards them in the hall.

'Ausweispapiere!' demanded the German, loudly. He wanted identity papers. I could understand that much.

I heard Mama respond with a polite, 'Ja, einen moment!' From where I was in our bed I could see her walk over to the drawer where she kept the papers that she had always known would one day save our lives.

I could see Mama fumble nervously around in the drawer and her body shuddered as the German yelled at her again. 'Papiere! Schnell, schnell!'

She found the documents and showed them to the German officer. But the German was clever. He knew the papers stated the bearer's place of employment. Mama would need to know the answer. 'Wo arbeiten Sie?' Where do you work?

For a split second Mama hesitated. No answer.

The German bellowed at her once again. 'Frau! Fragte ich Sie, wo Sie arbeiten?'

I couldn't bear this. I thought Mama would get the same treatment as Mrs Polonski. I prayed and prayed. Mama! Answer him, answer him!

Then the Ukrainian soldier looked at the document and read it aloud. 'Olindustrie.' Oil industry.

'Ja, Ja,' Mama answered, her voice quavering.

195

'*Olindustrie.*' She'd been saved by chance, by the Ukrainian's own words.

Mama continued to answer after that, as the soldiers asked her many questions. Surprisingly the soldiers never asked if anyone else was in the apartment and seemed to decide suddenly that they weren't even interested in Mama any more. They left in a hurry, thrusting the papers back at Mama, not even glancing towards the bedroom door.

Mama latched the door behind them as best she could, though the door didn't close properly now that it had been forced open by the soldiers. Then she replaced the papers in the drawer and returned to me in the bedroom. She leant against the door frame, utterly exhausted and very pale.

'Mama!' I cried and she came over to me and hugged me tight like she always did. It was only then that she gave in. 'Oh my God, Sala!' she sobbed. 'I was sure they were going to discover us! I was sure they'd guess I was Jewish. Those Ukrainians can just about *smell* Jewish fear!'

We held each other for a long time, waiting for the fear and the shaking to go away. Then Mama said at last, 'It wasn't just us who were lucky today, Sala. These people hate the Poles too. They could've just as easily killed the Poles in our apartment for hiding Jews.'

My body began to shake again. I could feel goosebumps form on my arms and a cold chill in my bones. I realised then how close many people in our apartment had come to being exterminated that morning.

And then Mama suddenly remembered...

'Oh God! Cilla! Cilla! I must go to her!' and she bolted from the bed and out of our apartment to see if Mrs Polonski was all right.

I wanted to run and help too. I wanted to see Mrs Polonski. But I couldn't make myself move from the bed. I wasn't worried about how badly Mrs Polonski was injured. I was worried Mrs Polonski might already be dead.

Later that week Mama discovered from her neighbours that the soldiers who'd stormed our apartment that morning had been looking for one Jew in particular, not just anyone. He'd been hiding in our building but had managed to escape barely half an hour before. All of us had been extraordinarily lucky. If he'd still been there the chances were that everyone in our building would have been rounded up and shot.

Mrs Polonski had been taken to hospital by one of our neighbours, bleeding badly after the attack by the German soldier, but after a week she returned home. We thought she'd recovered well and that our troubles were over, but we were wrong. The week of her return she knocked on our door and wanted to see Mama urgently. I was playing with Eva in our living room and overheard their conversation in the hall.

'I don't know how to tell you, Larissa, but . . .' Mrs Polonski began.

'Tell me what?' said Mama, and my heart began to race again.

'We're in *so* much danger. And you've got to fix it,' Mrs Polonski said.

'What do you mean by that? What do *I* have to fix?'

'The Gestapo were here, just this morning. They accused me of hiding Jews. He told me that he'd only let me get away with it if I paid him five thousand *zlotys*! In cash.'

'Five thousand *zlotys*!' Mama laughed. She walked over to the special drawer, took out our identity papers and slapped them angrily into Mrs Polonski's hands. '*Here!* I am not the one putting you in danger. We are not Jews! We have papers. So don't accuse me of putting you in danger. Not when I have risked *everything* to protect everyone around me. Who else is in this building? Perhaps you should check them instead!'

Mrs Polonski was completely taken aback by

Mama's fierce response. 'All right then! I will! But don't say I didn't warn you.'

Mama followed her out into the corridor, but before Mrs Polonski headed downstairs to speak to another tenant, Mama grabbed her quickly by the shoulder. 'And don't you *dare* accuse us, Cilla! Not after all our help. Have that much decency at least.'

I don't know how Mrs Polonski responded to Mama's angry words – all I could hear were her footsteps going down the stairs and Mama coming back into our apartment.

I was still playing chess with Eva when she came back in, and I'd been focusing on how to take Eva's queen when all of the commotion with Mrs Polonski had blown up. Now Mama came over to us, and I pretended to be in the middle of planning my next move.

'Eva, I am sorry, but I think it's about time you left.'

'Yes, Mrs Fein,' Eva said politely and began to get up.

'Mama!'

'No, Sala, I'm sorry, but Eva must go now.'

It was no good arguing. Mama was adamant. She latched the front door behind Eva and turned to me.

'You heard what Mrs Polonski said?'

'Yes, Mama.'

'Well then . . .' And to my great surprise she took a

small bottle out of her skirt pocket. She held it up to me and took me over to the dining table. She placed the small bottle on the timber surface.

'I don't understand, Mama. What is that?' I asked, but I was beginning to feel anxious again.

Mama looked distracted all of a sudden, as if her mind was far, far away. Then she looked up at me and said simply, 'This is cyanide.'

'Mama?'

'Poison.'

'What?'

'If they come looking for us again, if they discover we are Jews, we will not need to go with them to a death camp. Instead we can end it all – on our terms. These pills will help us.'

'But Mama!' I began to shake with fear and could not believe what she was saying.

'I know you want to live.'

'Yes! Yes, I do!'

Mama's face crumpled then. 'I don't want it to come to this either! But I will not let my son, my only son, suffer in a camp. I will not let you die like vermin. I vowed always to protect you, remember?'

'Mama! But this is not protecting!'

'Darling.' She softened then. 'Many others in hiding have pills too. Here, you can tuck them into your hair, like this, or hide them in your clothes. We only use them if we have to.'

I had no choice. I told Mama I'd keep the pills and learn how to tuck them into my hair to hide them. But I kept pleading with her not to give up hope. I'd never seen Mama so despairing. So much terror, so long living in hiding was making her do desperate things.

'I am running out of ideas. I don't know what else to do.'

'But Bella always helps.'

'I've asked her for so much, already.'

'But we've got this far. Please, Mama! Don't give up!' I was beginning to think that I was the one who'd have to be strong now, and I couldn't bear the look of pain in her eyes. Shame flooded through me. I had to get her to do something.

'Mama, pick up the phone and call Bella. She always knows what to do.'

So finally Mama did, and explained to Bella what had happened. I listened to her speak in a voice that didn't even sound like Mama, quiet and expressionless. 'We cannot survive any longer, Bella,' she said. 'They will find us. It is only a matter of time.'

There was silence. I could just imagine Bella telling Mama off for giving up. And then Mama spoke calmly. 'I know, Bella! Sasha has his whole life ahead of him. I *know* this, and I know I don't have the right to take that from him.'

Mama was becoming more and more distressed.

'All right, all right, Bella. I will get some rest. Perhaps you are right. By morning I will work something out. Perhaps it is not so wise to surrender, not just yet.'

But neither Mama nor I had a good night's sleep that night. The following day, Bella arrived in the afternoon and apologised for being so late.

'I came as soon as I could! Oh, Larissa!' she said when she saw Mama. '*Look* at you! Bags under your eyes, hair all over the place. Tears on your cheeks. This is not the Larissa I know. You are stronger than this!'

Mama simply burst into tears. She sobbed so loudly I thought she might die there on the spot. Bella took her into her arms and they stayed locked in that embrace for a long time until Mama was ready to sit down and talk. I just stood there – I had no idea what to do. Then Bella began to talk, quietly and firmly, like a teacher trying to encourage a student at school.

'Larissa, you have come *so* far with Sasha. You simply cannot give up now! *His* life. That *has* to be your focus.'

Mama seemed to gulp for air and swallow hard as

if a stone was stuck in her throat. 'But I am *scared*, Bella! So scared. I am afraid of everything I know and all the things that are unknown too. I am scared of what Hitler is going to think of next. I am scared about what they have planned for us now.' All the blood had drained from her face. All her strength had suddenly disappeared.

Bella turned quickly to me. 'Sala, my dear, please get me a drink. A proper drink. Whisky . . . you know where Mama keeps the whisky?'

'Yes, Bella.' I went to the cabinet near the dining table and brought out two glasses and the bottle of whisky that Wicek had managed to find for Mama on the black market.

Bella sat Mama down on the sofa and poured herself a glass. 'Well, I know *I* really need this and I think you do too,' she said to Mama in a cheerful voice, filling the other glass and handing it to her.

We sat in silence for a while, Bella finishing her drink and pouring herself another. Mama sat motionless, quiet, and eventually she too reached for a second drink.

'Well, Larissa,' said Bella eventually. 'The thing is this. You know I am a member of the Council to Aid Jews. Zegota. The Polish underground, the resistance. It's run by gentiles and Jews cooperatively. We started it in 1942 and we do many things. We provide Jews with money, food and medicine. Zegota operates in Warsaw, but it has around a hundred cells. Krakow has the second largest branch. And there are smaller ones in Wilno . . . and here in Lwów.'

Mama and I listened in silence. 'So, Larissa, my dear, through Zegota, I think I can help you and Sala. I've recommended you to the organisation. You can contribute to its administration, and you can help by creating false papers for your fellow Jews here in hiding.'

Mama looked astounded at what Bella was suggesting.

'Why are you looking at me like that?' said Bella, sounding quite surprised.

'How? How could you recommend me, without even discussing it with me first?' said Mama. 'You haven't asked me what I think about it yet.'

'Oh, for God's sake, Larissa! What's there to think about? You know you'd be brilliant at the job, and it will give you more income. More importantly you will have a chance to see beyond your own lives for once! You're not the only Jews in hiding, you know. Through Zegota you will be part of a bigger network, working towards the same goal. To survive! All of you! The survival of your *people*!'

The idea sounded exciting to me, being part of the resistance. We'd felt so helpless for so long. It made me feel that there might really be a chance for us to survive Hitler's plans. And maybe then I wouldn't have to wear stupid dresses any more.

Mama seemed to compose herself. 'Well, can you tell me more? What sort of people are working for Zegota? How can they be trusted?'

'Larissa, they are wonderful people working for us. You'll see. There's a Polish Catholic woman who heads the Zegota children's unit in Warsaw. She is amazing! I can't tell you her name, of course, but her father was a doctor who treated so many Jews who had typhus when other doctors wouldn't. He died of the disease when she was only nine, but she inherited his compassion and respect for all, Jews included. These are the people we work with, Larissa! The ones who remember their humanity.'

Bella poured herself another drink. I thought she should probably stop. Maybe she was just really good at holding her alcohol. Then she took out a cigarette, lit it, inhaled deeply, and paused. Mama looked at her, incredulous. 'Bella! Since when do you smoke?'

'Oh, you'd be surprised what I get up to these days!' Bella smiled and inhaled again. 'Actually,' she continued, ignoring Mama's look of complete astonishment, 'a friend in Zegota introduced me to smoking. But let me get back to my story,' she said, taking another puff and crossing her legs.

'Through this woman's work as an officer in the Social Welfare Department, she managed to get into the Warsaw ghetto, under the guise of inspecting sanitary conditions during a typhus outbreak. She managed to smuggle out around two and a half *thousand* children! Think of it. Two and a half thousand! Hidden in ambulances and trams, and then she placed them with orphanages – you know, rectories and convents and places like that – and we provided the false identity documents. It was brilliant!'

Mama and I were fascinated. We hardly ever heard of survivals. We just heard about all the deaths.

'Well, she certainly sounds like an amazing woman,' Mama said.

'She certainly is!' said Bella, taking another drag on her cigarette. 'But that's why we need people like you, to create those documents. And it will give you something to do and keep your mind away from useless thoughts of cyanide and giving up.'

'Are there others like her in Zegota?' Mama had become interested now.

'Of course,' Bella went on. 'Lots of wonderful people, so selfless. There was a woman who I shall call Rachel. We helped her when she arrived out of nowhere with her seven-year-old daughter. She'd been on the run, hiding where she could. Spent three months in Auschwitz and survived! Her daughter went to a convent in Lwów, where other Jewish children were hidden, and she's safe there now. Her husband, he was killed in Buchenwald.'

'Oh.' Mama sounded tired all of a sudden.

'But we managed to help Rachel and her sister too. Placed her in a wealthy Polish home, where she works as a servant now.'

Bella got up from the chair and walked around the room. She appeared to be looking for something and Mama noticed. 'Bella, is there something you want?'

'No, no! I just need to stretch my legs.'

Mama wanted to know still more, so she kept asking Bella questions and Bella kept on with her stories of hope and survival.

'And there was a woman doctor, a pediatrician trained in America. She came back when the Soviets first occupied Lwów, and we found a home for her where she worked as a cook at first, then became the family's physician. There were five children in that home to look after!'

'That's wonderful! But, Bella, I don't know. It's lovely to hear these stories, but me? Working for Zegota?'

'Larissa, our army founded Zegota to try and end all this madness. The Home Army, the *Armia*

Krajowa. It fights militarily, it provides intelligence information to the Allies, organises resistance, you know – sabotaging actions, planning assassinations of Nazis, destroying their military stores and fuel supplies. We damage their planes and vehicles, derail transport, blow up railway bridges.'

This was sounding good to me.

'And,' Bella continued, 'we deliver forged documents and money to Jews in hiding. It's very dangerous, of course. Some of our couriers are discovered and shot. Some are imprisoned, some tortured, but they never give anything away about Zegota. Some have been in Ravensbruck concentration camp and survived! But there, I shouldn't be telling you this . . .'

'Ravensbruck. That's a women's camp, isn't it?'

'Yes, for all sorts of women. There are more Poles, Russians, Ukrainians, German dissidents and Jehovah's Witnesses than there are Jews in there. Children too – Jewish and Romani. Damn the Nazis! You know they do experiments there?'

'What?'

'Experiments. On people – sterilisations, bone transplants, experiments with muscles and nerves, without any anaesthesia.'

'Bella!'

'They even infect wounds with bacteria and then

treat them with all sorts of drugs to see whether they can be cured or not. Things like that.'

Mama looked at Bella, utterly horrified. She looked at me, then back at Bella. I couldn't believe what I'd just heard either.

'Bella! Surely not? And, Sasha... do not listen to such things!'

'It's all true, Larissa. I'm sorry, Sasha, that you need to hear this. But now you know why survival is so important.'

My throat was dry and sore, and a lump formed in it as if I needed to cry but the tears wouldn't come. It was hard to know what to say about such horrors.

'But why all this cruelty, Bella?' Mama said. 'I cannot believe this. It is torture! Inhumanity! We are all *people*, we are all the same. Why would they do this?'

Mama became very upset then. She came over to me and took me in a hug and began to rock me back and forth, until Bella stood up and pulled Mama off me. She sat her back in her chair. 'Larissa, stop this. Stop it now and listen to me. I am telling you both, all of this, so you know the *truth*, so you know *why* you need to survive.'

'Why do we need to survive, Bella?' Mama said, sounding suddenly tired and defeated.

'You need to survive so you can tell the world

what these people have done. *That* is why we have to win.'

Mama looked up at Bella, then looked over at me. She sat silently for the next few minutes or so. So did I. Then Mama rose from her chair and wiped away the tears that were streaming down her face.

Bella spoke first. 'Larissa, are you all right now?'

'Yes, Bella. I am fine.'

Bella stood up, stubbed her cigarette out and straightened her skirt. 'So, can you see the bigger picture now, Larissa, my dear? We are fighting so much evil. The world must know.'

Mama looked at her and said nothing.

'You can be part of it, Larissa. Come on board with us! Join me at Zegota. Make a difference.'

Still Mama said nothing. After a while, Bella asked Mama one final question. 'Are you with us or not, Larissa?'

More silence . . .

'I am with you,' Mama said.

Chapter 15

THE LANDSCAPE OF WAR

The next few months seemed to pass slowly, and Mama became suddenly occupied with things I really had no idea about. She enjoyed it though; it seemed to give her strength, and once she'd joined Zegota and began working undercover like Bella, she became very different to the Mama I was used to. Now her task was to create new identities for people – false passports and birth certificates. And, except for Bella, nobody in the organisation knew that Mama was Jewish.

But she was so busy now, and I was getting bored. Even more bored than usual. I know it seems as though my entire life was pretty much just sitting around listening to the adults' conversations, and really that was just about it. There was nothing else to do. I couldn't go out. I only had a few books to read. I could draw sometimes, play chess with Eva occasionally, but most days consisted of boredom and sleep. And I still had to wear that dress all the time.

'I suppose Bella was right again, Sala! I didn't want

to join Zegota but I am enjoying this work. It feels good to help others.'

'Yes, Mama. It is good.'

'We must all try and help our fellow Jews. It is the only way for us.'

'Has Binka joined the resistance too?'

'Yes, oh yes! And Rena, and Wicek. Binka loves it. She's even met a man she likes. Alan, a wonderful man, a Polish gentile.'

'Is there any way the resistance can help rescue Aunty Mania then?'

'I do not know. It is difficult. I trust that she's still in hiding – somewhere – God knows, but it is too dangerous. I just don't know. One of her neighbours told me she was safe. Let's hope so, Sala.' But Mama became quiet after that.

And so the months passed, Mama busy with her resistance work, everyone around me busy, and me stuck with nowhere to go and nothing to do except read the same few books over and over again.

Months went by with no change, no raids, very little news from outside. There were rumours about Americans and invasion. I don't know how many months went by like this, three or four maybe. Six months? I don't remember. But things *were* changing outside. The adults were talking about it. Mama called it the landscape of the war. She'd heard more about the Polish *Armia Krajowa*, the resistance army. There were plans. Some sort of national uprising against the Nazis. The war was taking a different turn.

Everyone in Poland, the Soviets, the Poles, all of us, we just wanted to get the Nazis out, to end the German occupation at last. And then in about the middle of July – 1944 it was now – the Polish resistance army and the Red Army attacked and liberated German-occupied Vilnius. I heard the details from the adults as usual, and I knew Vilnius had been part of Poland before the war began. Now it would be Polish once more.

But while all this was beginning to happen outside, Mama heard other news in those desperately terrifying and at the same time hopeful months. She didn't say much to me, but I knew. I heard her whispering to Binka and Wicek. I heard the word 'Gestapo'.

'I am frightened, Binka.' Mama kept her voice low and thought I couldn't hear. But I'd become an expert at finding just the right place to hide and eavesdrop. 'The Gestapo, they are clever. They will hunt Bella, I know they will. They are on her trail, even now.'

'You cannot know that for sure, Larissa. And Bella is good at looking after herself.'

'But Lwów is becoming too dangerous. Bella could be arrested any second!'

'How? How do you know this?'

'Her supervisor at Zegota has ordered her to go to Warsaw. She is going to hide there, stay low. I think she's gone already. She didn't even have time to say goodbye! They wouldn't have done that unless things were dangerous. The Gestapo must be onto us.'

'Well, we can only find out bits of news, Larissa, and only through Zegota. I know you are worried, but you must have faith!'

Several more days passed after Mama spoke about Bella being in danger. Soon after, the weakened German forces left the city area of Lwów, but they stayed on the outskirts. They were gone from our neighbourhood, though, and through our bedroom window I could see no German soldiers at all now. Things were strangely quiet. It was a weird atmosphere, exciting in some ways because the tide of the war seemed finally to be turning, but Mama and I – all of us – we didn't dare hope too hard. We'd seen this before, and then things had got worse.

And we were right to think this way. A few days later, everything changed again. The Red Army rolled into Lwów.

We stood and watched from our bedroom window on that warm summer's day. I will never forget it! The

German forces had gathered once more in the city centre, and heavy fighting began again all around us. We were terrified and hopeful all at once. Perhaps this was the end of the German Army! Perhaps the Polish resistance army would be victorious at last! We'd heard that Polish forces had infiltrated the southern and western parts of the city, so anything could happen.

We watched and waited and listened from our apartment, not daring to hope too much, not thinking too hard, not getting too excited... I would watch sometimes for hours out of our bedroom window to see if there was any change, anything unusual happening out there on the streets.

Over four long days, beginning on 23 July 1944, the Polish resistance army and the Red Army rose up. They fought together, united against the Germans. And Lwów was finally liberated from Nazi control.

We stayed hidden, safe indoors, as much as possible during this time, just listening to the fighting, eating what little supplies of food we had, mostly tinned stuff Mama and Binka had stocked up on just in case. Mama tried to find out more about what was happening through her connections in the Polish underground, but her communication channels were blocked now and we heard very little of what was really going on. So we just sat and waited and slept... and prayed for it all to be over.

On another warm summer's day, a week or so later, at the end of July, I'd been dozing on our bed and must have fallen asleep, because I remember being jolted awake by a sharp burst of noise coming from outside. Mama had been lying beside me and she jumped up and pulled the curtains open.

'Mama? What can you see?'

'In the street below... Sala! Oh! There are *tanks*! Many of them!'

'Tanks? What sort of tanks? *Panzers*?'

'No! No! Soviet tanks! Come and look!'

I got up and joined her quickly at the window. Yes, many tanks; large, immensely heavy Red Army tanks moving through our city. Mama opened the window wide and a sudden burst of cheering and shouting met our ears.

'What are they saying, Mama?'

'"Freedom! Freedom!" They are shouting, "Freedom!" Oh, Sala! At last, at last!'

There were crowds everywhere, so many people, more people than I'd ever seen in one place in my life. People everywhere. So many that we could not see the pavement or the street underneath their feet. And the noise was deafening! So much excitement – happy screams, cheering, laughter, and smiling faces and tears of joy. At first I couldn't take it in. There was too much going on. It was too different from the quiet, tense days of hoping against hope. This couldn't be real! But I watched as the crowds surged down the streets. I picked out a boy on the streets below who'd knelt down and kissed the muddy boots of one of the Russian soldiers. Then the crowds surged around him once more and he was lost to my sight amongst a massive sea of moving bodies.

A wave of relief washed over me as I began to realise what was happening and what it all meant. Mama leant on the windowsill beside me and sobbed and sobbed and waved, and blew kisses into the air.

'Mama? Mama, what are you *doing*?'

'Sala! Don't you *know* what this means? The Soviets are here! They have driven out the Germans!'

'So the Germans are gone? *All* gone?'

'Yes! Yes! They are shouting it outside. Listen! The war is won.'

'Won?'

'Yes, Sala! Won! We are saved!'

It took me a while to grasp what Mama was really saying. I'd lived with war for so long. I'd forgotten what *not* living in a war was like. I didn't know what to say, so I asked the first thing that came into my mind. 'Can I go outside then?'

'Yes! Yes, you can, Sasha! But wait!'

'What?'

'We have something important to do! For *you*,

Sasha! We'll go and see Wicek. I'll ask Wicek. Come on!' And she grabbed my hand, laughing and as full of joy as I had ever seen her.

Hearing my real name 'Sasha' stopped me. I felt as though I was hearing my name for the first time. It was weird. I had got used to being called Sala. 'Ask Wicek what?'

'Let's go to their apartment! Come on!'

Mama ran from our bedroom, unlocked our front door and quickly ran next door to Wicek's and Rena's, with me following behind, not knowing what Mama was even thinking.

We found Wicek, Rena and Selena glued to the window of their place just as we'd been, and they too were watching the commotion in the streets below, the groups of Soviet Red Army soldiers wandering through the streets, amid the immense crowds. Vehicles were everywhere, blocking the way. People still crammed the pavements and found it difficult to walk through the streets at all. I'd never seen so many soldiers, shabby worn-out soldiers, nothing like what I'd imagined the proud conquerors of a city would look like.

Rena and Selena started to jump up and down with glee when we walked in. They ran over to me and Mama and hugged and kissed us joyously. Very soon, Binka and her Polish boyfriend, Alan, also joined us, all of us laughing and crying at once and hugging each other.

Then Mama grabbed my arm and took me over to Wicek and whispered something in his ear. She was smiling and laughing as though she knew of a great secret or a joke or something that she wanted to tell me but couldn't.

Wicek looked at me and smiled too. 'Come with me,' he said and led me into his bedroom. Mama followed, and Wicek began to search through a chest of drawers, where he quickly found a shirt, a pair of brown trousers, some underwear and some shoes.

Boys' clothes.

'Here, Sasha,' he said, laughing. 'You might need this belt in case the pants are too big for you. But they'll do for now. At least it's not a dress!'

I stared at the clothing and had no idea what to say. I picked up the crisp white shirt and hugged it. I could feel tears starting to well up inside me. 'A man's shirt, a real man's shirt,' I mumbled. It was all I could think of to say. Then I put the shirt down and picked up the trousers. I stroked them and could almost not believe that they were to be my clothes. I turned to Wicek. 'Thank you! Thank you so much!'

I looked down at the dress I was wearing. I might have hated it, and I still did, but it was so familiar now, so ordinary. I felt a choking sensation in my throat.

I tried to smile at Wicek. 'I can't believe... can I really wear men's clothes now? Is it safe already? I don't have to be a girl any more?'

'No, Sasha,' Mama said, almost in tears herself by now. 'No more Sala. You can be a young man now.'

Wicek gave me a slap on the back. 'Off you go then! Now change!' And he and Mama left me to it in the bedroom.

I began by unbuttoning the dress. As it fell to the floor, limp like a rag, I stared at it, and Wicek's words echoed in my mind: 'Change,' he'd said. Like peeling off a skin, like shedding a layer and becoming something else underneath, a caterpillar changing into a butterfly. The choking sensation returned to my throat. I was relieved to take the dress off, of course I was, but it was the strangest feeling I'd ever had. It swept through me like a tide of shame, or joy, or fear – I didn't know what. None of these things and all of these things. It felt so strange to let the dress go after all those years of wearing it, of hiding my life behind it. I thought of Eva. What on earth would she think now? She would realise she had undressed in front of a boy instead of a girl that day in the bathroom! That she had been naked in the bath with a boy.

I thought of how much I owed to something as simple as this dress: it had been my saviour, the focus of my undercover existence for all this time. I'd relied upon it around the clock, every waking moment and every time I had any contact with any human being. And now suddenly, it was no longer needed. Tears began again.

I bent over to touch the discarded dress one more time. My cover, lying there on the ground. Just like that. A sense of attachment, of ownership, suddenly came over me, something completely unexpected. All I'd ever felt for this hideous dress was utter disdain, complete revulsion, but now I saw it as something quite different. Now I no longer needed it, I was able to feel appreciation for its role in saving me.

Wicek came back in to see how I was getting along. He quickly picked up the dress and threw it on the bed. 'Hurry up, then! It's time to change, young man!'

That word again. Change. 'What will we do with the dress?' I asked, not knowing what else to say.

'Well, you won't be needing it again. I think that dress can go in the bin! It's certainly not for you any more. Time to move on, my boy!'

Move on. Was it that easy? But with those words from Wicek echoing in my ears, I realised then what this really did mean. It meant that this liberation was real. The war was really over, and it had brought us freedom. But not just liberation from the Germans, not just freedom for all of us. For me it was a very special kind of liberation. There was freedom to be me, to be my true self – a man. I'd waited so long for this moment and now that it had arrived, it felt completely foreign.

I now had to be a young man, nearly an adult man. I couldn't take it all in, not all at once. The change was too great, too sudden. And the tears came flowing down my cheeks.

The war was over. And Sala was gone.

PART THREE

AND ME

Chapter 16
SALA IS GONE

That was how I ended 1944. By going from being a girl to being a boy again. I had a lot to get used to.

After the dress, the second casualty that day was my hair. Wicek took me in hand once more. 'Come on, Sasha! You can't get rid of the dress and still have that hair!' He shoved me into the bathroom, took a pair of scissors from the vanity drawer and wasted no time. He sliced off most of the long locks around the sides of my face and began to trim neatly around my ears and the back of my neck. I closed my eyes for most of it and could feel the cold metal of the scissors' blades as Wicek worked quickly and with a great deal of concentration.

When he finished, I opened my eyes and looked at the image in the mirror. Me. Was it me? *Really?* I could not believe what I saw. My face was so pale, and it looked sharp and angular now without the long curls to soften the edges of my cheeks. I looked completely unfamiliar. I was almost mesmerised by my own reflection and I couldn't tear myself away.

'So, what d'you think, Sasha?' Wicek said. 'The new you, eh? Or the old you, really.'

There I was, in boys' clothing, and suddenly I looked like I had a male body. I had no waist any more. The hair had made the biggest difference, so it hadn't just been the dress that had changed the way I felt about myself. It had been the hair too.

I looked at the tailored pants . . . I'd forgotten what they felt like. A dress had been so loose around my legs and now trousers just felt tight and uncomfortable.

Wicek leant on the door frame, crossed his arms and smiled as he watched me in the mirror. 'Well, I'm no hairdresser, Sasha, but you'll be able to go to a proper barber now and get your hair cut just like all the other boys, first chance we get! For now, come on, let's go outside and see what's going on! Freedom, eh?'

Mama had stood quietly by the door while Wicek had cut my hair. She hadn't said a thing, just watched while I turned from being a girl back into being a boy. I wasn't even a boy, though, not really. I was a young man. I'd been a girl for around two years. Now I wouldn't have to shave the hair on my face so carefully, and it didn't matter that my voice was deeper. When I turned around to look at Mama she gasped. She looked at me almost as if I were a stranger.

'Sasha, it is a metamorphosis! My Sala has become my son!' She had tears in her eyes, and she came over to me and laid a hand on my shoulder. 'Thank you, Wicek, for giving me my boy back at last.'

'Well, come on then!' Wicek almost shouted. 'Join the celebrations!' And he slapped me on the back, something that no one had done for years. He took Mama's hand and mine and led us out to the rest of the family in the living room.

But by the time we got there nearly everyone was outside or at least running down the stairs and out into the streets. In the commotion they didn't notice me, so Wicek and Mama and I followed behind, all of us piling out of the apartment block with everyone else from our building. Our neighbours were all out there already, Eva and her mama as well.

Oh God, I'd forgotten about Eva. I wasn't ready to face her as a boy. And I was sure she wasn't ready to face me as a boy either.

Eva was the first to notice, though and when she saw my short hair and trousers she just stopped in her tracks and stared, her mouth hanging open in total disbelief.

'Sala?'

'Yes, it's me.'

'But... but...' In that instant we'd both switched off from the celebrations all around us.

'I know,' I continued. 'It's a bit of a shock, right?'

'But... you're a *boy*!'

'Yes. I can explain...'

'But...'

'I know – it was all part of a plan, to disguise me while the war was on...'

But Eva wasn't really listening.

'Sala? You're not really Sala?'

'No, I... but it's all right... really.'

'It's not all right!' Eva sounded angry.

'What?'

'But you're a *boy*!'

'Yes...'

'I had a *bath*. With a BOY!'

'Eva, I'm sorry about that, but I had to protect myself. I was sort of undercover as a girl.'

'But the bath!'

'Well, we thought you were a bit suspicious. We thought if you saw me in the bath you'd be convinced that I was a girl. We were scared you might say something and if the Gestapo found out...'

'But I *undressed* in front of a boy! Stark naked!'

'Yes, well... I am sorry.' I tried to imagine how Eva must feel.

'How *could* you? Sala, we were friends!'

'Well, it's hard to know what to do, in a war and everything...'

Eva wouldn't look at me after that. She'd gone bright red and turned abruptly round in a huff, and went to join her sisters. I felt bad that I had hurt her, I didn't want to. And it was horrible now to lose a close friend.

I realised then that I hadn't been taking in the thousands of people everywhere shouting and laughing, crying and celebrating in the streets all around me. The noise grew and grew. I stuck by Wicek and Mama, tried to enjoy the sense that the Germans had been defeated at last, but it was no good. All I could think of was that all around me were my neighbours and Mama's friends who'd thought I was a girl and now ... one by one they began to stare at my clothes and my hair.

Eva's mother Cilla came, looked at me and then at Mama and she was clutching her chest as if she was about to faint.

'Cilla?' Mama said, and grabbed me by the hand. I think Mama was afraid Cilla would do something to me, tug my hair to see if it were real or something ...

'Well!' Cilla gasped. She was utterly astounded. 'I knew all along that you were *Jewish*, but I *never* imagined that Sala was a boy! Never in a million years!'

This time it was Mama's turn to be shocked. 'What? But Cilla! How on earth did you know we were Jewish?'

'I just knew! Of course I knew! I couldn't say anything, but I knew.'

'But *why* didn't you say anything?'

'For goodness' sake, Larissa! Zegota! We share the same goal. And we're both mothers. Don't you think I'd understand about protecting our children?'

Mama looked confused and amazed. 'But I don't understand! Why did you try to bribe me then? Why did you ask me to pay those five thousand *zlotys* to the Gestapo?'

'I had a cover too. I had to pretend to be what I'm not. You mean you really didn't know who I was? You really thought I'd turn you in?'

'Well, I had no idea. I thought you just wanted money from me.'

Cilla threw back her head and laughed. 'Well, I *was* convincing, wasn't I?'

'Yes, you certainly were. Oh, but it is Liberation Day! We must forget these things and celebrate,' Mama said, and we laughed and hugged and cried some more, standing there amongst all the crowds and crowds of ecstatic people on one of the most momentous days in our history.

Much later that day, when the mass of people had finally broken up and most of the families began to go back to their homes, Mama and Cilla continued that conversation about Zegota. Cilla had come over to our apartment, but Eva still wasn't talking to me and didn't turn up with her mama. It was a quieter, more subdued afternoon. I was glad for that.

'We'd been watching you, you know,' continued Cilla. 'How you behaved and reacted in various situations. Not everybody can join our organisation. We have to be careful. And so we watched everything you did. I can't believe we didn't notice Sala, I mean . . . Sasha, though!'

Mama nodded. She went quiet for a moment and then said calmly, 'Cilla, seeing that you're in Zegota too, and must have links to other groups in Zegota, well, would you know anything – anything at all – about what happened to my sister Mania? The last we heard she was hiding in a cellar somewhere in Brody. We tried to get her out, but every time I was told it was unsafe.'

Cilla hesitated.

'Well?' said Mama.

'Actually, Larissa, I do know.'

'Oh, Cilla! Really! You must tell us!'

But Cilla looked very anxious and I didn't like the way she hesitated. I'd seen that look on people's faces before. Mama and I prepared for bad news once more.

'Your sister *was* hiding in a cellar, yes. But Brody

was overrun by Germans. She was in hiding the whole time she was there. When the Soviet tanks moved in she must have thought it was safe, as many others did. When she came out she'd been holding the hand of a little boy, we were told. He'd lost his mother earlier in the war and Mania had taken him in. I think the child was around six years old.'

'Oh, but that is lovely! Some company for each other,' Mama said, sounding bright all of a sudden.

Cilla didn't smile back.

Mama gasped then and I went over to Mama and put my arm around her shoulder.

'Go on, Cilla,' Mama said quietly. 'Please, tell me more. I need to know.'

'We were told... well, quite suddenly apparently, out of nowhere, two Wehrmacht army officers arrived the day everyone thought it was safe to come out at last. The Soviets were on the other side of the building your sister was hiding in...'

Mama grasped my hand and made me sit beside her at the table. I could still hear people laughing and celebrating outside in the street.

'Well, it seems there was a Pole standing near the German officers and he started yelling, pointing his finger at your sister, saying, "*Zydowa, Zydowa.*" Jewess! Jewess!'

Mama went pale and asked in a whisper, 'And what happened then?'

'I am sorry, so sorry, Larissa! One of the Germans went over to your sister, and he eyed her up and down, and then looked at the boy. Of course he told the boy to drop his pants.'

Tears sprang into my eyes when Cilla said that. It was what Mama had always feared would happen to me.

Cilla went on. 'And of course your sister told them she wasn't a Jew. Of course she did. But it was . . . too late by then.'

Mama took a deep breath and clutched even tighter at my hand. 'And so she was shot?'

'I'm so sorry, my dear,' Cilla said in a very quiet voice. 'It would have been very quick.'

Tears rolled down my face. So my Aunty Mania was now free. But not in the same way as my other aunties. Mama and I should have been rejoicing that afternoon. We should have still been celebrating like the others in our apartment block. But instead a sharp stabbing pain took over in my heart. Liberation Day had changed. It should have felt so good, so sweet. Only minutes ago it had. But now a sense of overwhelming guilt came over me. Here I was, sitting at our dining table in our city of Lwów, alive, while Aunty Mania and that little boy were dead. Zayda was dead. And now Aunty Mania too.

It was around this time that the nightmares began. I'd sometimes had bad dreams about Germans and Ukrainian soldiers, and I knew Mama had also had nightmares about Zayda. But now for me the nightmares got worse. Sometimes I felt as though I was physically dragged out of bed, or that I couldn't breathe, or that I was shouting, 'Don't shoot! Don't shoot!' but no sound would come out of my mouth. And then I would wake, my pyjamas drenched in sweat, and the terror of it all was overwhelming.

Other dreams began then too. Dreams about being a girl, where the 'me' that I knew suddenly disappeared and I was replaced by another person, a girl I didn't know at all. I had this dream many times after Liberation Day. I dreamed about my hair growing longer and longer, and then Wicek coming along with giant scissors and cutting off my head as well as my hair. I would always wake from these dreams in a cold, cold sweat. And some nights I didn't want to go to bed at all because I was too afraid of what I would dream that night.

So now a large hole had taken the spot where my heart should have been. I thought of Aunty Mania looking after that little boy. A little boy like I'd been once. How easily that could have been my fate. I could have been caught so many times in the previous few years. I would have missed seeing Liberation Day. I would have missed an entire lifetime.

I had escaped by a miracle. By a miracle, by my mama's immense determination and by a hideous striped dress.

Chapter 17
LIFE IN GLIWICE

Even though I'd waited for liberation for so long, I wasn't prepared at all. It was new in so many ways. It wouldn't be Hitler's world for a start. And it wouldn't be a girl's world for me. I wasn't prepared for being a young man in a world where everything was suddenly completely different.

The Germans were gone from our part of Poland, it was true, but the war still went on in other areas and it wasn't until May 1945 that the Germans finally surrendered and the war in Europe came to an end for everyone.

But the world I'd known for so long *was* the war. There was nothing else. It was an existence of fear and uncertainty. It was about running and hiding, survival and deception. All of us were the same. Except for one thing. It was different for adults. I was nearly ten years old when the war began. And now I was struggling to remember what life had been like before. I was so used to hiding my Jewish identity and my gender that it was very hard for me to believe that I could now live freely and be completely open about who I was. Lots of the kids around me were the same – confused. No wonder we had nightmares.

And there were so many things we were still struggling to find out. Mama and I desperately wanted to know where Bella was. The last we knew she'd left for Warsaw, and that had been over a year ago. Since then we'd heard nothing.

'I miss her so much, Sasha!' Mama said one afternoon when we'd been talking about Zegota. 'I wonder where she is, if she is safe! She was such a big part of our world. And so dear to me. In all the terrifying chaos of this war, dear Bella was always so reliable. It feels wrong to be celebrating the end of the war without her. And I cannot believe she wouldn't survive. Not Bella. She was invincible!'

I thought that probably didn't make any difference. Invincible people could still be blown up by bombs. But I didn't say that. Instead I said, 'But Mama, there is no way to contact her.'

'I know, Sasha. But we must not forget her. Not ever. We must pray and hope there is a way.'

Before long, the euphoria of being liberated from the Germans gave way to the reality of daily life. While we were no longer fighting for our lives, and I wasn't in disguise, life under the Soviets wasn't easy. There was no more income from Zegota, so Mama needed to find a job. But she was luckier than most. She went back to the company she'd worked for before the war and got a job as a personnel officer. That was perfect for Mama. Her knowledge of Russian wasn't as good as her Polish or German, but it was enough. Soon she started work and, like the days before the war, Aunty Binka came to stay.

'I am *so* glad to be back at some normal work,' said Mama to Binka. She was smiling while she tidied some knives and forks into the cutlery drawer. 'And the office is a good place to work. The building isn't bad – not too damaged. Except for the lifts, of course. They've all been destroyed, so I have to walk up ten flights of stairs to get to my office. Think of it, Sasha! I will get very fit!'

'And tired,' said Binka, who was always very practical.

'Yes, well . . . the salary could be more I suppose. We've barely enough to buy some bread and a little butter. I'll have to think of a way to earn some more, and in the meantime we will just economise. At least we are used to that.'

But Mama knew economising wouldn't be enough. There was never enough money left over to buy anything other than basic food, and she was worried that I was still too thin and undernourished. We'd heard about people selling vodka at the food market and making lots of money. But she needed money up front to buy the vodka before she could sell it on at a profit.

'We have no cash! But we still have some of Bubbe's linen that I kept during the war. Some women will pay good money for nice linen, won't they, Binka?'

'I expect you can sell it for a good price, Larissa,' said Binka. 'Enough to buy the vodka anyway.'

'But the linen is all we have left of Bubbe's,' I reminded them, and immediately thought of Bubbe's precious locket that had been used to buy our false identity papers.

'Sasha, we need to be practical,' Binka added. 'The war may be just about over, but not yet the hardship.' I knew she was right. But I hated seeing the last of our family possessions being sold off. We used to have such nice things before the war, and all of a sudden I thought of Zayda's chess set and the little silver horse that Mama used to have. My horse.

But it was no use. At daybreak on the following morning, Mama went straight to the market to sell Bubbe's linen, and soon after that she was able to buy enough vodka to start selling it in the market. She was now in the alcohol business. She didn't quite know how the system worked, though; none of us had any idea about the black market. It was all so new to Mama, and so I went along to help.

Very soon after we arrived at the market on the first morning, and we'd set up our own small stall with bottles, a pair of young Polish girls approached us.

'Vodka, you're selling?' one of them asked. She was blonde with wide-set eyes.

My heart was beating fast. I wished she'd asked Mama instead. But I smiled and said, 'Yes, we have vodka.'

'Six bottles, please,' said the other girl.

Mama and the girls agreed on a price and the two girls carried the bottles away. It wasn't long before we'd sold all of the vodka we'd bought that morning. I was beginning to think Mama had sold it too cheap.

'Well, that *is* a relief!' said Mama. We returned home with our cash, me to stay with Binka, and Mama to go off to the office for the rest of the day.

Mama and I returned to the market the following morning with a new set of bottles. But the very same girls from yesterday approached us once more. Only this time they were not so friendly. The blonde girl raised her eyebrows and said to Mama in a nasty voice, 'What did you think you were doing yesterday? Don't try to fool us! Your vodka smells of petrol!'

Mama gasped. 'Well, I . . .'

'You just be careful! The Russian militia will be

looking for you. They don't like people who cheat us out of the real thing. Just remember you could be arrested for this.'

I was terrified. Mama made some sort of excuse, but as soon as the girls went away, she bundled our remaining supplies up and we headed straight for home. 'Oh God, Sasha, I had no idea the vodka was tainted.'

'Can you take the bottles back, Mama?'

'Well, the rest of them – I'll try. Yes, I think I will have to.'

So Mama took the bottles back to where she'd bought them from and told the man about the petrol. But he didn't care. Mama lost money over that deal, and she never sold vodka at the market again. Instead she sold sugar. 'At least I can taste that and I can tell if it's not the real thing. I will stick to things I know about from now on,' she said to me, and I thought that was a very good idea.

From then on I stayed in the apartment when Mama went out selling on the black market. Binka hadn't found work yet, though she was looking, and in the meantime ran the household, just like old times.

Mama wouldn't let me try to find work. 'Don't be silly, Sasha! You are far too thin. You will be safer at home still.' But she did better with the sugar, and we were soon able to buy more food. But there was something even better than that! With the extra money I was allowed to buy one or two books. Books at last! Something to break the boredom! So I began to teach myself some history, some geography and to read a little literature. I even began to read Mama's copy of *Anna Karenina* that she had slipped into her case without me knowing. Life was immediately better.

We stayed in Lwów until the end of May 1945, when Germany finally surrendered and the war in Europe was over. Really over. But Mama could see that life in Lwów was going to remain difficult, and she knew we needed a fresh start. So in her usual determined way she announced to Binka and me what we would do next.

'We will go and live in Gliwice, Sasha! I have heard all about it. People say it is lovely, the last major city of the Third Reich.'

'Where?'

'On the border between Poland and Germany. Upper Silesia. It's been under Polish control since the end of the war. Oh, how much I want to begin again, Sasha! Somewhere else, anywhere but here! Anywhere as long as it is away from where we've had to hide for so long. Lwów holds too many memories for us now. In Gliwice, I can find work and you will be able to go to school at last.'

School? It was so long since I'd even thought of school. I wanted so much to learn, but I was nervous about the idea of school now. I didn't know anything. And I'd have to make friends again. I wondered if Eva and her sisters felt the same.

And so Mama made plans to go to Gliwice. In earlier times, Gliwice had been part of the Hapsburg Empire. I'd been reading about it in one of my history books. At the radio station there, in 1939, the German secret police had simulated a Polish attack. Mama said that was partly used to justify Hitler's invasion of Poland at the start of the war. 'Hitler was nothing if not devious,' she said.

But now Gliwice had a reputation for being full of Germans who insisted that they had no idea what had gone on during the war. 'But don't worry,' Mama reassured me. 'Most of the Germans are leaving Gliwice now. The Poles are moving there, people just like us. We will be at home . . .' And she smiled broadly and went to find our suitcases.

The day we arrived in Gliwice, carrying our two small suitcases of belongings, we walked down Zwyciesta Street from the railway station to the market square, passed the wooden radio station tower, passed the remains of cafes, restaurants and fabulous shops, and old buildings once topped with ornate steeples and archways, fine roofs and façades. It was a cool day, with thick clouds above and a few drops of rain beginning to fall.

We were walking through ruins. The once beautiful buildings now had their windows and doors boarded over, their people gone, more casualties from this long and deadly war.

Mama and I arrived at the market square and stopped for a moment in the shade of a broken wall. I tried to picture the city as it might have been in the thirteenth century, a glorious trade and craft centre with merchants bargaining for cloth and hops and flour in bustling city streets. There'd been a drawing of that in one of my history books. Now there were just factories where the Germans had made coal, iron and steel. We were happy to learn that Jews still lived and worked here, though we were not sure if the synagogue and the Jewish cemetery were still intact.

We wandered around a bit and then rested again in the market square. 'Sasha, I am not certain it was the right decision to come after all.'

'Why, Mama? We've only just got here. We'll find somewhere to stay.'

'But it is all so unfamiliar! Perhaps it was a mistake

to come to a place where we have no friends. Perhaps we should have stayed at home with Binka.'

'No, Mama, we will be fine. I can start again as a boy now. No one here will know I had to be a girl once. I like that much better. In Lwów I was always bumping into people who kept making comments about me as a girl. I hated it!'

'Well, yes, there is that I suppose.' So then Mama picked up her suitcase and said with a determined tone, 'Off we go then, Sasha! Let's find our new home!'

Our new home became a small apartment close to the centre of town that Mama found through a group of people helping to relocate Poles whilst many of the Germans were being expelled.

Gliwice was very different from Lwów. During the war, Jewish men and women in Gliwice had worked as slave labourers, producing ammunition for the Nazis in one of the four sub-camps of Auschwitz-Birkenau. In other camps they worked repairing railroad vehicles, or maintaining machinery, or they helped make coal tar. Military production had dominated everything, and the Jews were used as labour.

Mama said this town had a feeling of sadness and defeat about it. 'It is struggling to move on from the death camps and the destruction, Sasha.' But at least Gliwice was trying to recover, and Mama and I could begin to enjoy some freedom. We could walk around without fear. We could breathe the fresh air without looking over our shoulders. It was wonderful. And we met many Jews and soon found a local community around our new apartment building. Then, over the next few months, Aunty Binka *and* Aunty Rena, and their families also came to live here. Even Selena. Poor little Selena who used to chant, 'Sssh Sssh, the Germans will shoot you!'

Now our lives were busy. Mama began to work at the market selling rugs. On most days, I helped her by carrying the rugs to the market. She'd buy them from the Germans and then sell them at a profit. Better than vodka and sugar. Mama chose not to think about the fact that she bought from Germans. 'I do not like it, but it is necessary. We must build ourselves a new life.'

Now my spare time was spent with my aunts once more. Mama still felt a terrible guilt about Mania, but we were coping in our new world of freedom. Now I was fifteen years old, nearly sixteen. Childhood was over. My boyhood had been surrendered just to survive. I'd spent much of my teenage years as a girl.

And there were still the dreams. Terrifying recurring nightmares. Ukrainians plagued my sleep almost every night. I could see their boots and smell the stench of alcohol on their breath, and I would wake up in a sweat, the fear of that day returning in an instant.

To help me cope, I began to take my football to Chopin Park, a leafy grassy area amongst some cafes and terraces, close to the market square. I'd kick the ball around just like I used to with Sam and Walter. We'd received a letter from someone who'd known them that last month. There was no trace of Walter now. He and his family had vanished. Sam's family had gone into the ghetto but never came out. I pulled my hair when Mama told me I would never see my friends again. Mama had been right about the ghetto in Lwów.

I'd run straight to the park the day I'd found out. I had to do something, kick a football, anything . . . and I yelled Sam's name so loud my lungs felt like they'd burst. I kicked the football as hard as I could, for Walter and Sam's as well as for me. Eventually I had to stop because my lungs hurt and my legs felt like jelly. I slumped to the ground and put my head in my hands. I'd bought that football new when we moved to Gliwice . . . it made me think of Sam every time I kicked it.

At first it felt strange being able to play freely in the open air. The first few times I'd look around and hope no one else was there. I had to 'practise' being a young man now. I'd look down at my sports shirt and shorts and wonder if I looked like everyone else. I was terrified I still walked like a girl. Maybe I did! I tried to stop doing all the feminine gestures and ways of talking that I'd adopted for so long. So I didn't talk to others much if I could avoid it. I didn't really talk to Mama much now either.

But one day after I'd been kicking the football around I went into the cafe opposite, near the market square. It's a day I'll never forget . . .

There was a waitress there, a Swiss girl who looked about the same age as me. I thought she was beautiful. Tall and fair-skinned with blue eyes and curly ash-blonde hair. When she smiled dimples would appear. I began to talk to her in those cafe visits, and she began to get to know me. Her name was Adriana.

I didn't tell Mama about Adriana. But Mama caught me one day when I'd just got home, before I'd had a chance to close my bedroom door. 'Just a minute, young man,' she said.

Great. If she called me 'young man' it was going to be difficult.

'I saw you today in the cafe, talking to the waitress there.'

I crossed my arms in front of my chest. 'So were you spying on me or what?'

'Don't be silly, of course not, Sasha. Did you have a nice time?'

'Yes,' I snapped. 'Mama, I'm tired and going to have a rest.' I went to my room and closed the door, and Mama gave up trying to talk to me that afternoon.

One Sunday a few weeks later I was kicking my football around Chopin Park again, when I heard Adriana call my name.

'So you like a bit of a kick, hey? Do you follow Polish football?' she asked. I doubted Adriana was really interested in football, but I played along, hoping she was really more interested in me.

'Ever since I was little,' I said.

'My grandfather followed Pogon Lwów,' Adriana said. 'Now I watch Cracovia Kraków and Ruch Chorzów. I guess Ruch Chorzów won more games before the war, but we'll have to see how they play now.'

Wow. I was impressed she knew so much about football. Then as we were talking, a girl ran past after a ball. She was dressed in what appeared to be boys' clothes and it startled me, a girl in boys' clothes.

'What's the matter, Sasha?'

'Nothing . . . just never seen a girl play football before.

Adriana laughed. 'Oh, Sasha, lots of tomboys do that.'

'Tomboys?' I asked.

'You know, a girl who likes to do boyish things. Like football.'

I thought of me wearing a dress and doing the opposite, a boy doing girl things. I wondered if there was a name for that too.

Adriana caught my attention again by placing her hand on my arm. 'I don't live far from here,' she said softly. 'Would you like to come to my place?'

'Sure,' I said, but my heart thumped in my chest and I didn't even want to think what Mama would say if she knew.

Adriana's apartment was about fifteen minutes walk away. She opened the bulky front door of the building and walked quickly up the flight of stairs to a first floor apartment and led me in. It was tiny, barely furnished – one small living room, a kitchen and a bathroom.

The first thing Adriana did was light a cigarette. Her red lipstick smudged over the tip. She flicked back her hair and passed the cigarette to me. I'd never had a cigarette before. Mama would kill me, but I took a drag and the pinch in my throat made me cough.

'Here,' Adriana said, and showed me how to do it. 'You know, there's a first time for everything,' she grinned and her eyes met mine as she passed the cigarette back to me. She took the cigarette and dropped it into the ashtray. I was beginning to think things were getting too complicated now. I liked Adriana but...

Suddenly she was kissing my neck. None of this was new to her. Not like me. I had no idea. I wondered where she'd learnt it all.

Adriana laughed. She looked at me curiously. 'So, what's the story with you and your mother? Where's your father then?'

'He died when I was two,' I said quietly.

'That's too bad. My parents were killed in a car accident when I was fourteen. I stayed with my aunt and her husband for a while, but then I ran away. I've been here ever since.'

I was shocked. I'd never thought of a girl having to live by herself. All the women in my family always had plenty of sisters and aunts and other people around them.

'Well, you do what you have to do to get through, you know?' She took a deep breath. 'Do you get on with your mother?'

I'd never really thought about it. 'I've been with her all the time. She's always taken care of me... So, yes... I guess so.' I wanted to say more, but couldn't. I thought of Mama, always there, always caring, always determined to save me during the war. This all felt like it was too much. I thought of Zayda and of what he used to say to me.

'You're lucky,' said Adriana. 'At least you have someone watching your back. I wish I had a mother who did that. Mine didn't care.'

I was silent.

'You're lucky. Having a mother like that,' Adriana repeated, as if it were the most important thing she'd said all day.

For the next two months Adriana and I spent afternoons together. I told no one about it. It was the first time I'd kept a secret that was truly my own. I really felt I was falling in love with her.

But one Sunday afternoon, we were meeting as usual, sunlight shimmering through her blonde hair, and she looked at me and I could tell something wasn't right.

'Sasha,' she said softly. 'I have something to tell you. I've met someone in the cafe. I told you about him, remember?'

'I remember something about a friendly man coming to the cafe.'

'Well, yes, his name is Salek. He's Polish.' She paused. 'I've seen him a lot these last few weeks. And well . . . I'm going to marry him.'

I stared at Adriana.

'Don't look like that, Sasha. I'm going to marry him because he promises to take care of me.'

'But . . . do you love him?'

'That has nothing to do with it,' she snapped.

'What do you mean, nothing to do with it? It has *everything* to do with it!'

'Love is just irrelevant, Sasha. I've never had anyone watching my back. *You* should understand. Your mother's done that for you all your life!'

My eyes blurred with tears. 'But that's different.'

'No, my dear, it is not.'

There was just silence. Until I asked, 'When?'

'Next Sunday. And I won't be working in the cafe any more, so we won't see each other again I'm afraid.'

So that was it. I couldn't speak. A sharp pain began in my chest.

'Look, please understand . . .' Adriana said softly.

I understood. I understood very well. I looked into her eyes. 'And so what were *we*?'

Adriana looked stunned. She didn't utter a word. And the pain in my chest was too great. I had to leave. I looked at Adriana for the last time. I could not even bear to say goodbye.

I ran to the park. I knew I couldn't go home, not like this. I felt like a fool. Tears streamed down my cheeks, and then came the sobs.

Chapter 18
DISPLACEMENT

I cannot begin to describe the emptiness and the hurt. For weeks I didn't feel hungry. I couldn't sleep. I went to the market alone. The park was my salvation when I wasn't working with Mama. I stayed away from her as much as possible, and kicked my football when the weather was clear. If I stopped kicking the ball for even a moment Adriana immediately came back into my mind. I missed her. How could she not miss me? But the worst thing was the sense that I had been used and had been so stupid as to think I had instead been loved.

One evening when I got home, Mama called out to me. 'Sasha, you are so late. Please, I need to talk to you.'

'Can't it wait till tomorrow?' I snapped. I snapped a lot these days.

'No, my darling. I need to speak to you now.'

'What, Mama?'

'Are you all right?' she asked, looking very concerned.

'Yes, just things on my mind.'

'But I want to know if something is wrong, Sasha. You're very jumpy these days.'

'I told you! Nothing, just stuff. Anyway, what did you want to tell me?'

'Well, I've had an idea,' she said, and I was glad she seemed to be changing the subject. 'I am going to Warsaw to find Bella! And you and Wicek can help me.'

'Me? But Wicek can help, can't he? Why'd you need me?'

Mama looked appalled, and I realised what I'd said.

'How can you ask that, Sasha? How *can* you? We are both alive because of Bella! Do you not think we should at least make the effort to find her?'

'Yes, Mama. Of course. I'm sorry. When did you want to go?' Actually I thought it might be good to get away for a while. It would take my mind off Adriana.

'As soon as possible, my dear. We can leave the market for a while. People will come back for their carpets later – they won't miss us for a few days.'

I took a deep breath. I felt guilty. I said, 'Well, we can ask Wicek tonight and then we can work out when to go.'

Mama looked pleased then. She probably thought I'd grown up all of a sudden.

The next week Mama, Wicek and I left for Warsaw.

Before the war, Warsaw was called the Paris of the East. It was a sophisticated city. Some of my papa's relatives had lived in Warsaw, and Mama sometimes told me stories about them. And now I could see their city for myself. I was looking forward to it.

But I would be bitterly disappointed...

'Oh Sasha!' Mama said when she saw the first streets of Warsaw and its grand buildings. Or at least the places where the grand buildings had once stood. 'There is nothing left! I knew it had been badly bombed, but *this*!'

It was true. My papa's beloved Warsaw was now a city of ruins. He would have turned in his grave, as Mama said, to see Warsaw like this. A city of such cultural richness reduced to dust and rubble. We walked through street after street of bombed-out ruins. Only the classical façade of the grand theatre remained; the beautiful building of the once-famous philharmonic orchestra utterly destroyed by Nazi bombing. This was a tragic city now, a city of death and cold winds and displaced lives.

Many Jewish people had lived here once. Mama said Warsaw had boasted the largest Jewish community in Europe, second in the world only to New York City. There were Yiddish, Polish Jewish and Hebrew publications, and many boys were still educated in *cheders* in a rabbi's own house, and there were many Jewish schools too: Mama knew a lot about my papa's favourite town.

We walked along to Tlomackie Square. Mama said there used to be a beautiful synagogue there, but this too had been blown up by the Germans. She walked me past the remains of smaller prayer houses clustered around the square, passed the Nozyk Synagogue in Twarda Street on the left bank of the Vistula River. I thought it must have been a wonderful place for Jewish people once. It reminded me of Lwów.

'But the city of Warsaw had its poor Jews, too,' said Mama. 'And many merchants, and there was a charming street called Ulica Nalewki in northern Warsaw, in the Muranow district. I don't suppose there's much left now.'

We walked on through the streets and Mama continued to tell me and Wicek of the Warsaw Papa once knew. 'There was a conversation I had with our neighbour Sima once,' she said. 'Her family had lived here too. She described Nalewki as "Rushing, always rushing!" Nobody looking – people pushing, always on the go. So much traffic. And it was about credit. People running from one store to the next to get short-term credit so they could pay their bills. Then the rush to the banks before they closed at three o'clock. Jews would be praying on the run, she said. Horse-driven cabs on the move. You could buy all sorts of goods – buttons, cotton, ribbons, lace, lingerie, furs, shoes – you name it! Oh, I'd love to have seen Nalewki! But now look at it, Sasha. All gone!'

'But Larissa,' said Wicek, 'think of Bella . . .'

'Yes, of course, we are here to find Bella.'

But still, even as we walked along the streets, it was impossible not to look at the destruction and think of what had happened. We were approaching the Muranow district now. There was nothing of it, just levelled buildings and rubble, but this had been the Warsaw Ghetto. Thousands of Jews died there, of typhus, starvation, extermination. Thousands more, thousands upon thousands, in the Warsaw Uprising when the Jewish Underground smuggled grenades and other weapons inside the ghetto and rose up against the SS. It failed but still, someone had finally resisted the Germans. It gave Jews throughout Poland courage to resist the Nazis in other ghettos too so that they no longer passively accepted their fate. I will never forget the day I walked passed the Warsaw Ghetto. Mama had tears in her eyes. 'Never forget, Sasha! Never forget!' she said.

We walked on. Mama didn't know at all where in Warsaw Bella might be. She thought our first stop should be the Zegota headquarters in Zuravia Street.

Perhaps meetings were still held there, perhaps they knew of Bella.

So the next day we walked to the Zegota building. It was a warm day and the sun was shining. Mama, Wicek and I found the street and knocked on the door of number 24. A bearded man opened it. 'Can I help you?' he said, and smiled.

'I am looking for a Bella Kowalski. I am a friend of hers. She helped me in the war. I need to find out if she is still here.'

'Bella Kowalski? I don't think there is anyone by that name here, Madam, but let me check. Do come in,' he said politely, and he eyed us up and down, perhaps surprised that anyone would bother to come to Zegota now.

The man ushered us into a small but comfortable sitting room and disappeared, leaving Mama, Wicek and me standing there, not knowing what to expect. We noticed a woman wearing spectacles over by the corner, busily typing behind a desk. She smiled and pointed to some chairs.

Mama took a seat and turned to Wicek. 'Do you think she could *really* be here?'

Wicek shrugged. 'I don't know, Larissa. It is a very long shot.'

Mama looked at me then, wanting reassurance. I didn't know what to say, and just shrugged like

Wicek. I wanted to find Bella too, but this place was so quiet. It didn't seem as though Bella was the sort of person to hang around in a bombed-out city if she didn't have anything useful to do.

I tugged nervously at my man's shirt, wanting to take it off. And then suddenly I felt like running again. Running away, as far away from here as I could get. It was agonising sitting and waiting for news.

We must have waited for about fifteen minutes, I suppose, though it felt a lot longer. Then the man with the beard returned. He didn't look encouraging.

'I am sorry, Madam,' he said to Mama, 'but apparently Bella Kowalski is no longer in Warsaw.'

Mama tensed. 'By no longer here, do you mean dead, or just gone from the city?' Mama knew to get straight to the point these days.

'We cannot confirm if she is dead, Madam. All we know is that she left shortly after the liberation.'

'Do you know where she went?'

'I'm sorry, there is nothing more I can tell you,' he answered firmly, almost dismissively. Mama knew there was no more she could do.

'Well, thank you for your trouble,' Mama replied and motioned for us to leave. That was the end of our investigations at Number 24 Zuravia Street.

'Where to now?' I asked once we'd got outside.

'I have an idea,' Mama said, suddenly much brighter. 'There was a fruit and vegetable kiosk that used to secretly operate as a Zegota branch. It was run by a friend of Bella's. They used to hide papers and money, even Jewish children in there.'

'Oh Mama, don't be ridiculous!'

'It is not ridiculous. Anything is worth a try,' she said seriously. She strode down the street, so Wicek and I had no choice but to follow. But when we got to the spot where she'd heard the kiosk used to be, there was nothing but rubble – like most of Warsaw.

'Larissa,' said Wicek gently. 'We could search for hours, days, with no clues. We must be realistic.'

Mama was almost in tears by now, though she knew Wicek was right. 'I think we have to go back to Gliwice, don't we? There is nothing for it. I don't know where else she could be.'

'I'm sorry, Mama,' I said, hugging her tight like she once did to me. I saw only disappointment in her eyes. She squeezed me tight and sighed, 'My darling boy!'

We returned to Gliwice that night on the train.

It was only years later that Mama would discover the truth. Bella had long gone from Warsaw, just as the man at Zegota had said. By the time we'd arrived in Warsaw looking for her, Mama's wartime saviour had been living safely in London for months we learned a little later.

After the war, Israel recognised non-Jews who saved the lives of Jews during the Holocaust as 'The righteous among nations'. Both Wicek and Bella were recipients of this honour for their underground work in Zegota.

Bella migrated to Israel in 1963 after losing her husband and spent her last years alongside those she had saved during the war.

Life in Gliwice changed after that, though. Perhaps it was seeing the mess of Warsaw that changed us. Perhaps it was the futile search for Bella. Whatever it was, living became more difficult. Selling goods at the market didn't ensure a steady income. Some days nothing was sold.

But what was far worse was that anti-Semitism was beginning to rise once more. We saw the signs – whispering, pointing fingers, dirty looks. One day a Polish woman at the market pointed at Mama and said, 'Look over there. At *those*! So many bloody Jews still alive and breathing our air! They should have been exterminated like all the others.'

We began to be frightened again. Memories of the war were fresh. It was terrifying to think that there were still people around us who would have been happy to see us die.

'I don't think we can be safe in Gliwice any more, Sasha. We'll have to move again.'

'But where?' Not that I didn't want to move. I had other reasons for wanting to go. I wanted to get away from where Adriana was living. I knew I'd be happier then.

'Well, we have very little choice, Sasha. If we move, we move to a displacement camp.'

So that was it. It wasn't very long until all of us left the border town of Gliwice, early in 1947, to enter the Pocking Displacement Camp.

The Pocking camp was in the United States zone of Germany, near the border of Austria. It had been set up in 1946. There were hundreds of other such camps in Germany, Austria and Italy – all over Europe, to cope with the flood of refugees from the war. The camps housed millions of people, including survivors of the concentration camps who'd been freed by the Allied armies and had nowhere to go.

And so we all settled in to a new life once more. Living conditions were not very good in the camps, but we had to make the best of it until we could be relocated to a better place. Mama and I shared living quarters in a large wooden military barracks with many other refugees, surviving now on tinned sardines, canned vegetables and biscuits provided by the United Nations relief effort.

Sometimes Mama would amuse herself imagining what she'd eat if she had a choice. One afternoon, she imagined freshly roasted potatoes with garlic and onions, cooked with chicken the way her mother used to do it. 'The tantalising flavours, the lovely smells wafting out into the garden I played in as a child, and the white curtains blowing in the fresh air...'

This wasn't helping at all. 'Mama, you are just making it worse. I'm starving!'

She came back to reality with a jolt and looked around our small, bare room. 'Sasha, my darling, we have come to this again! So little food, just wretched sardines or biscuits with powdered coffee.'

'Well, at least we have something. There were times when we had nothing, Mama. And we're still together.' I managed a smile. During my whole life, there'd been hunger one way or another. I remembered times when my belly had ached with emptiness. Tinned food would've been most welcome then. We'd survived far worse than this. Here we were safe. The camp at Pocking didn't have fresh food or good sanitation, but it didn't have German soldiers or bombs either.

And Pocking had one thing I'd never experienced before – a thriving Jewish community. Those who wished to re-establish their Jewish practices could do so here. There was a rehabilitation and training programme, so people in the camp could learn new skills. Then they could use those skills in the outside world once they left Pocking to start a new life. They could learn lots of things – auto mechanics, corset making, dental technology, dressmaking, electrical engineering, joinery, radio technology, working with leather... There was also a clothing factory in the camp where people worked making suits from military material. Mama was energised. She chose to learn dressmaking.

While Mama was learning to sew, I spent my time reading, trying to catch up on all the gaps in my education. And then Mama met a new friend at dressmaking – the sick wife of a highly regarded doctor who'd held an important position in Munich before the war. Her name was Irena Hansen, and she'd been separated from her husband when a bomb exploded in the hospital while he was at work. She'd been at home at the time and she hadn't seen her husband since; she didn't even know if he was alive.

Mama mentioned one day to Irena that she was thinking of going to Munich so that I could get a more comprehensive education. She'd heard that a new Jewish community was forming there. It might be the fresh start we needed.

Irena seized the opportunity. 'Larissa, please,

I'm too sick to go, but could you... would you take a letter, for my husband? Please? If he is still there, still alive... Here, I have written to him.' She handed Mama a small, very worn envelope.

'Of course I will, Irena.'

'I just don't know what else to do!' Irena cried.

Mama hugged her and reassured her that she would do what she could.

It seemed just about everyone in the world was trying to find someone who was lost.

Mama took the letter and tucked it safely into her pocket.

Chapter 19

MUNICH – AND MILA

The following week, Mama and I were on the move again. We left the Pocking Displacement Camp, this time for the city of Munich.

Once again this was a city of rubble. Munich had been badly damaged by the Allied bombing. Even its beautiful Gothic cathedral *Frauenkirche* had taken a severe beating. I wondered if the Christian God had anything to say about this. Once again I thought of Zayda. 'God will be there to guide you,' he'd said. 'In the bad times you must always turn to God.' Munich and Warsaw must have had a lot of people who weren't so convinced about this now. I wanted to trust Zayda's words, but I looked at these ruins and wondered – where was Zayda's God when these beautiful buildings had been blown into rubble?

Mama and I made our way, over the course of the next few days, to Schwabing, on the northern outskirts of Munich. Nearly three quarters of Schwabing had also been bombed. Was there anywhere on earth now that didn't look like this?

The war had destroyed so much. Even the survivors, the people walking past us, looked as though their souls had been destroyed. How were they meant to keep going? How were Mama and I meant to keep going? How was I supposed to have faith, like Zayda had said I should, after all that Hitler had done?

Mama interrupted my thoughts then with some cheerful words about Irena. 'She is so proud of her grand city, Sasha. She grew up here. She said Schwabing used to be the artists' quarter, you know! Oh, thank goodness she gave us directions before we left.'

We were trying to find the hospital where she hoped Irena's husband might still be working. But the city had changed so much, and many of Irena's directions didn't make sense any more with half the recognisable landmarks destroyed and streets with no names and piles of rubble blocking many others. 'Oh, Sasha, I don't know which way to turn,' said Mama in desperation as we tried to navigate our way through yet another bombed-out neighbourhood.

I thought it was time I started to take charge. Mama looked exhausted and I could see she was about to give up. 'Let's ask for directions then, Mama. Here – inside this shop.' And I went into a small grocer's to see if they could help us find our way. It turned out we were not very far from the hospital at all.

'It's all right, Mama. Come on, we'll go this way!' I took her hand and led her further along the street. We walked another block, then another, and came to the street Irena had told us about. And there it was – *Krankenhaus Schwabing*. The 98th General Hospital. And it seemed quite intact. There was some damage to the front walls, shrapnel marks and that sort of thing, but otherwise the hospital had survived miraculously well.

We went nervously through the front entrance and asked a nurse at the reception desk if there was a Doctor Hansen working here. It was a busy place, a number of doctors were bustling around and patients were being admitted, but the nurse we spoke to was helpful and seemed relieved that she didn't have to admit us as patients.

'Well, of course,' the nurse said. 'Doctor Hansen is free, I think. Shall I show you to his rooms?'

'Oh my goodness!' said Mama when we realised how easy it had been. We'd been expecting another dead end, another commiserating person giving us bad news. But instead the woman cheerfully directed us to where the doctor could be found. 'I can barely believe it! Oh, I wish Irena were here. She must know, as soon as we can tell her.'

I smiled at Mama, took her hand and led her through the corridors in the direction the nurse indicated. We found the doctor's room easily, and another nurse came over to us and asked if she could help. Mama explained our mission, and the reaction of the nurse was instant. 'Well, in that case you must wait here!' said the nurse, smiling. 'Do sit down! I will bring him straight away. This is such good news,' she said, and gave Mama a hug.

Almost at once the nurse returned, pulling a man by the hand while she beamed furiously and brought him over to where we were waiting. He had snow-white hair and glasses, and was dressed in a white overcoat. He looked puzzled about all the fuss. He looked at us sitting there as though we were something he'd never expected. 'Please, come into my room,' he said, ushering Mama and me in, shaking his head and looking utterly bemused.

'I am Mrs Fein, Doctor Hansen. I've come all the way from Pocking to see you. I have wonderful news.' And she handed him his wife's letter.

'My dear God!' he said as he immediately recognised the writing. 'My Irena is alive! My *dear* God!'

'We came as soon as we could. She wanted us to find you . . .'

The doctor had tears in his eyes by now and hugged Mama and me and, when he'd recovered enough to actually talk, he said, 'But how can I ever thank you!

And I have to get her out of Pocking. I must.' And then, 'Oh, but why did she not come herself?'

'She was too ill to travel, Doctor Hansen. But she is getting better, much better! And we are happy to help. I am sure you can get her home very soon.' Mama smiled reassuringly.

'Is there something I can do for you, my dear, in return?'

'Oh, do you mind very much, Doctor?' Mama said immediately. 'There is one thing I need, something simple. Do you think you could examine us? We've been living on canned food for so long in the camp and our health, especially my son Sasha's here...' She looked at me and I wished she hadn't looked so eager.

The doctor smiled broadly. 'But, of course, my dear! Such a simple thing when you've come so far for me and my wife!'

And so we were taken in that day by the doctor and thoroughly examined. He organised tests for us and told us how we should begin to look after ourselves again, what food we should eat. 'Both of you have some toxins in your blood – from the canned food. It is quite usual. I will supervise a cleansing diet for you this week. This means a liquid diet only, of fruit and vegetable juices to begin.'

I gasped. 'Mama! Do we have to? I starved enough

during the war! Why do we have to starve again on a stupid diet of juice.' I tried to whisper so I wouldn't offend the doctor, but the last thing I wanted was less food. The thought of a week in hospital drinking nothing but juice was horrible.

'Sasha, the doctor said,' said Mama, embarrassed. 'When the toxins are gone we can have solid food again. It's not the same as in the war.'

I wasn't convinced. I was glad when the days of juice were over.

We'd been at the hospital just over a week and before we left, Doctor Hansen asked Mama if there was anything else we needed. 'Anything at all,' he said. 'I'm so grateful for your kindness.'

Mama was unwilling to ask another favour but the doctor insisted and in the end Mama was defeated by her desire to help me. 'I want my son to have an education, Doctor Hansen. He missed so much school in the war, you understand. I don't know if you know of anyone...'

'Well, of course, Mrs Fein!' he said cheerfully. 'Let me think... I have some connections at the *gymnasium*. Let me see what I can do.'

And so Doctor Hansen used his connections at the high school to get me a place, and he even organised extra tuition because I'd missed so much and was very behind. I was looking forward to school now. I'd been reading so much and I wanted to get back to some real learning.

In the weeks that followed, Mama and I once more found new accommodation in a new city, only this time I could begin to settle into a school as well. I was so busy. Being in a new school reminded me, of course, of Walter and Sam, how we'd fool around in class and kick the football in the schoolyard or the meadow after school. I constantly missed them, but now I had so much learning to do that I didn't want to spend time making new friends. I just wanted to make up for lost time and so much lost learning.

The school I went to now wasn't far from home, in an old red-brick building down a series of bombed streets and opposite a park. Mama had found us a new apartment, a good place to live, with a small backyard and a room I could call my own bedroom at last. We'd spent only a little time back at Pocking, enough to tell Irena of the wonderful news and enough to get organised for yet another relocation.

Trying to study again was hard, though. My mind was constantly distracted by memories of Adriana and old friends and Zayda. One afternoon I jotted down some points on a sheet of paper. I decided to write a letter. I thought carefully about what I wanted to say, and began like this:

```
Dear Adriana,
I am studying hard and feel lucky to
have a chance to learn at last. We
are in a new apartment. I am learning
to read and write in German before
I can work on the curriculum. It is
difficult. Once I master it, I will
learn Literature, Latin, History,
Geography, Mathematics, Chemistry,
Physics, Biology, Geography, Art
and Music. I am also learning
English . . .
```

I looked at what I'd written so far, scrunched up the letter and threw it in the bin. What's the point? She dumped me. It's over. I had to study now. This wasn't the right time for me to be worrying about love. I got out my school books. That afternoon, while Mama was out, I did nothing but study.

Mama didn't return until late that afternoon. She looked happy when she got back. Unusually happy. 'Mama,' I asked, 'What's going on? You look like something wonderful has happened.'

'Well, yes! In a way. I just met an old friend.'

'Who?'

'Misha! Oh, you don't know him, Sasha, but he was my brother's very best friend, all those years back in Brody. We went to school together. Fancy meeting him now. Just in the street like that.'

'So did you invite him here?'

'Well, no, not yet. It was such a surprise!'

I suddenly conjured up an image in my mind of Mama as a young girl, running around together with her brother and school friends, laughing and playing, with no war and no starvation. I could see why Mama was so happy. We were surrounded by strangers in this new city. To find someone she knew by chance was nothing short of miraculous. I wished I could just bump into my old friends from school like that. Samuel and Walter were always on my mind.

'We sat and talked for a while in the park,' Mama went on. 'He's a little stouter than I remember, of course. Older, with grey hair now, but he's the same Misha. Such a familiar face! He just called out to me in the street! "It's Misha!" he said. So we swapped addresses and he'll come and see us soon.'

I really hoped he would. Mama needed friends too, now that Bella was gone and her sisters were in other places...

We knew Rena, Wicek and Selena were now in the Feldafing Displaced Persons Camp in Bavaria. It was a better camp than many, and close enough for us to visit. Rena wrote to say she was happy there for now – the camp provided education and entertainment, and they even had a theatre and an orchestra. Many people there were Hungarian Jews, Rena said, and they'd already made friends with another Jewish family, the Hirsh family from Poland.

Rena mentioned the Hirsh family a lot in her letters. There was Masha Hirsh and her two daughters, Kasia and Mila.

In the next few weeks Mama and I were able to travel by train to see Rena. Mama was ecstatic. And on our second trip there I first met Mila Hirsh.

Mila was the same age as me. She was standing in the doorway of Rena and Wicek's barracks as Mama and I walked up to the front door.

Mila was a quiet girl with long, black hair right down to her waist and chocolate-brown eyes. I couldn't take my eyes off her. She was amazingly pretty. Aunty Rena must have known something, because she wasted no time in introducing us.

'Sasha, darling, I want you to meet our neighbour here, Mila,' she said. 'Mila, this handsome young man is my nephew, Sasha.'

'Hello,' Mila answered, with a lovely smile.

I didn't know what to say, so I just stood there and smiled back. Hopeless, I thought.

'Actually, I've seen you before,' Mila said. 'Over on the stairs talking to Wicek last time you came to visit. I remember your brown suede jacket.'

'Oh,' I said. Even more stupid! I had to think of something to say. 'Why are you dressed in a white uniform?' I asked then, and immediately thought that sounded like the worst thing I could've said in the entire world.

She laughed. 'Well, I work with the dentist here in the camp. He's teaching me German, as well as dental nursing. I'm sorry, I have to go now because my session is about to begin.' She smiled at me once more. 'See you again, perhaps!'

'Yes... um... I look forward to that,' I said in a sort of stammer. I went straight to ask Aunty Rena about her after that.

'She's staying here with her mother and sister, Sasha,' Aunty Rena told me. 'They are Polish Jews, like us, from a town called Wolozyn.'

'Oh,' I said, trying to sound casually interested but not so keen that Rena would suspect I was really really interested. But I needn't have worried. Aunty Rena seemed to want to tell me all about Mila anyway.

'One night, Russian soldiers came to their house and took their father away. It was at the end of 1939, or maybe it was early 1940, I can't remember. But the girls were left to fend for themselves with their mother, poor things. They won't talk about what happened.' Rena sighed. 'Like lots of people,' she added.

That day we didn't stay long and I didn't see Mila again until the following week. But I began to think about her a lot, and suddenly Adriana slipped from my mind. All that week at home I found it hard to concentrate on my studies. I kept seeing Mila's pretty face – her beautiful dark hair and enchanting eyes.

That same week Misha, Mama's friend from her school days in Brody, had got in touch. I liked Misha. He was a happy, stocky man with hazel-brown eyes and light-brown hair that was going grey and thinning on top. I liked him because he was a very practical person. He saw life the way it is, no frills, no fantasy, he said. 'That's how you make money, Sasha! By being practical. By buying land. By getting an education. One day you'll make it in life, Sasha, as long as you study hard and you are good to your mother.'

Misha began to visit us every day. I was pleased. Mama needed a friend, and now Misha was here she was much happier and she worried less about me. It was as though something wonderful had fallen from the sky for us. A gift. Perhaps Zayda's God was there after all.

The next week we travelled to the Feldafing camp again. I was, of course, hoping to see Mila, so this time I combed my hair carefully. It was so thick these days that sometimes the comb got stuck and actually broke in my hair. That hadn't ever happened when I'd had longer hair as Sala. I cringed. I pushed that memory away. I tried to look especially nice when I went to visit Mila.

This time I found Mila in Aunty Rena's room, both of them chatting as though they'd known each other forever. It was a beautiful summer's day too. Everyone was happy.

'Hello!' I said, and then thought I'd sounded way too cheerful and wished I hadn't grinned so stupidly when I'd walked in.

'Hello, darling,' answered Rena. 'I'm so glad you're here. But I really must run and find Wicek. Something important has come up. I'm sure we'll catch up later,' she said, and then she disappeared.

Well, that was a bit obvious, I thought. I knew she'd left deliberately. She'd worked out that I was very interested in Mila.

I looked at Mila and smiled. 'Shall we go for a walk?'

'Yes, it's a lovely warm day. Not even hot yet.' Mila smiled back.

'My aunt mentioned that you're here with your mother and sister,' I began.

'Yes, just the three of us.' I could see the sadness in her face then, and hear it in her voice. I wanted to ask about her father but didn't know how.

'What about you, Sasha?'

'Oh, nothing much to tell. I live with Mama in Munich. I'm going to the *gymnasium*.'

'What about your father? Your Aunty Rena never mentions him.'

The question surprised me. I sometimes almost forgot that I'd had a father. 'He died when I was two, a long time before the war. I never really knew him.'

'I am so sorry,' she almost whispered. 'I was nine when my father was killed. That was bad enough.'

We walked on through the camp and around the buildings, just wandering really with no place to go. 'My mother brought me up,' I added. 'Actually . . . it must have been hard for her.' It was the first time I'd really thought about that.

'Yes, very difficult,' Mila said.

I was quiet for a moment. Now might be the right time to raise the question. 'And your father?'

Mila hesitated. 'He was killed at the beginning of the war. By the Russians.'

I didn't know what to say about that. Instead I asked, 'Where were you during the war then?'

Mila didn't answer straight away. 'I prefer to forget really. I'd rather remember my home before the war.

My father had a flour mill and my sister and I would ride on the wagons. He didn't really allow it. He was afraid someone would get hurt. We did it anyway, though, only when he wasn't looking!' She laughed. 'But let's talk about you instead.'

'There's not much to tell. I had some friends at school, Sam and Walter. Walter seems to have disappeared and Sam didn't survive in the ghetto...' I changed the subject. 'And I'm sorry I didn't have more time with my father. My mother adored him. She always talks about him, even now. She says I'm a lot like him.'

'Well, that's a good thing, isn't it?' Mila smiled.

'Maybe.' There was an awkward pause, so I tried to change the subject again and asked about her sister instead.

'Oh, she is married now.'

'What? Already?'

'Yes, Kasia met her husband Rischek in the previous camp where we stayed, Schlachtensee, in Berlin. He was on the committee in charge of food. He knew lots of high-ranking officers and could get vodka and cigarettes... almost anything. He even had a jeep and a driver. Rischek was *crazy* about Kasia. And the wedding. Our mother prepared food for three hundred and fifty people. Imagine that! It was in a large hall where we used to have dances on

Saturday nights. The musicians in the band were American and Polish, and there was even a table of high brass American military. The party didn't end until six in the morning. We danced, and ate and drank all night. It was wonderful, Sasha!'

I was amazed to hear that there was even enough food in a camp to feed that many people, let alone prepare a wedding feast.

Mila went on. 'We lived in barracks there too. There were many blocks, around fifteen to twenty rooms in each. We had to share a toilet and bathroom with other families, which I didn't like much. But we had regular dances, and musical evenings and even performances on stage. There was a school, and you could learn dressmaking...'

'Like my mama.'

'Yes, and metal trades, radio and dental technology... that was my interest. And we had a rabbi with us in the camp too.'

'A rabbi? Well, I'm done with all that religion now,' I said, perhaps a little too quickly. In the last few weeks I'd finally decided I'd had enough of God.

'But why? Because of the war?'

'Yes. Being Jewish is important, of course it is, but I don't want to be observant any more. I'm not even going to fast on Yom Kippur now. I've gone through too much starvation to do that. I never want to feel hungry again. Weren't you hungry in the war?'

'Yes, but... my family remains observant. We will continue to fast and still believe in God, not as a being, but rather a force, an energy of some sort. That's how I see God. And, Sasha, it wasn't God that created the war, but Hitler – a crazy power-hungry man.' Mila stopped to draw a breath. 'Anyhow, that's all past. I want to look forward to the future now.'

What she'd said about her family reminded me of Zayda. I looked at Mila, and then glanced down at my watch. 'It's getting late! I have to catch the train back to Munich. I'll walk you back to the barracks.'

In a way I was glad I had to go. I'd wanted to talk, but too much talking about religion made me sad, and it was too beautiful a day to ruin it by too much of that talk.

Back in Munich I had exams coming up. But Mila was constantly on my mind. She was different – sweet and kind and a breath of fresh air. She made me start to think about my future. I wanted safety, and work, and one day maybe a family of my own, and love. I wanted to build a life. Nothing more than that.

But the war was not so easy to escape.

One night that week, after studying late, I'd fallen

asleep with my books open on my bed. I'd woken suddenly, in a cold sweat, and flashing before my eyes were the Ukrainian soldiers again, standing before me clear as day, dressed in their crisp uniforms and heavy boots, shouting at me in Polish: 'How long have you been living here? Where is your mother?' Beads of sweat trickled down my forehead and fell onto the crisp white sheets.

She abandoned me, I wanted to shout. She left me all alone. My own mama!

I began to whimper like a small child. And tears started to stream down my face. I knew Mama had just panicked that day. I knew she loved me. But I couldn't shake off the thought that she'd also left me. That it had been only sheer luck that had saved me. Not Mama. Mama had left.

I suddenly felt incredibly alone.

I sat up in bed and stroked a hand across my face. I needed to shave. I immediately thought of the days I had to shave and pluck every single hair out so I would look like a girl. I remembered how hard it had been to walk like a girl, to talk and behave like a girl. But what had been hardest of all? I realised then that the most difficult thing of all had been to find the strength and the will to survive at all, to get above the constant, unrelenting fear that was always there. And to trust. Who could we trust in those dangerous times? We were lucky with Bella and Marysia.

I sighed deeply. And then, the thoughts of being a girl flooded back again. I'd never felt like a girl inside. I'd done my best to *look* like a girl, but it was just a performance. And that made me think of Mama. I could see that she was happier now she'd found Misha. Maybe I'd be happier too, now I'd found Mila.

Mama's secretarial skills had by this stage landed her a job in Munich, but she spent most of the weekends out with Misha. He was a warm, kind fellow, and I liked him a lot. He and Mama went to movies together, enjoyed strolls together and sipping coffee in the cafes. I didn't know whether Mama loved him, but I could see that she was very comfortable with him, and he seemed to accept her headstrong, determined nature. I was glad they got on so well.

The weekend after my exams were over, I took the earliest train I could to Feldafing and Mila. When I arrived she was waiting at the front of the camp, smiling and waving. 'Sasha, you are just in time for lunch. Your aunt has something special for us!'

I smiled back. 'Good. I'm starving!'

'And after lunch . . . I have a surprise for *you*!'

'Really?' I had no idea what she meant.

'You'll see!'

So a little while after lunch, Mila took me outside and led me out of the camp and over to the river. 'Come on! It's so warm and sunny. We're going kayaking!' And her eyes lit up brightly at the idea.

It was the most perfect afternoon I'd ever had. Kayaking in the fresh air together, and a long walk in the park afterwards. We talked and talked. And I told Mila everything – all my life – the fear, the dreams, the hunger – and the masquerade. My mind was like a black abyss on some days. But slowly that afternoon I began to unravel my whole life story. Mila was mesmerised. I pulled out a photograph of me as a girl that I'd brought with me, and she gasped. Tears welled up in her eyes. 'Oh, Sasha!' she said. 'I had no idea!' and she took me in her arms and hugged me tight.

At that moment I looked into her eyes and drew a deep breath. 'Mila . . .' I paused again, not knowing quite how to say this. 'I think I have strong feelings for you now.' I thought I sounded ridiculous but didn't know how else to say it.

She hugged me again. 'Sasha, you silly boy!'

'What?'

'You have nothing to worry about at all.'

'I don't?'

'No! After all, I have those same feelings for you. Didn't you know?'

I broke out into a warm smile then, took her in my arms once more and kissed her for the very first time.

Chapter 20
A NEW LAND

After that wonderful day together, Mila and I saw each other every weekend.

Usually, I went to Feldafing, but occasionally Mila came to see me in Munich. I loved her so much. This time it was real. Adriana had been a first experience, a first way of opening up, but it wasn't the same. I could think of nothing else but Mila: her beautiful, musky hair against my cheek, the touch of her skin, her bold, brown almond-shaped eyes. But most of all it was her sweet nature that I loved. I'd never seen that in Adriana. She'd been tougher, harder. She'd had to be with no one to watch her back, like she'd said. Maybe that had made all the difference.

So much happened in those few months in Munich. Not the least of which was this – Mama finally married her childhood friend Misha.

The wedding was held in a small synagogue, one of a few still able to perform services. Mama didn't want a fuss, so the wedding was small and life went on as usual after a simple service and family celebration, but everyone attended – me and Mila, of course, all

Mila's family, Rena and Wicek, Selena, Binka and everyone. Friends from the camp and friends from Munich. Our new world was finally beginning. Lives were falling into place.

And me? Now I felt that I was finally growing apart from Mama – in a good way, though. I was working out a life of my own. We'd been together, just Mama and me, through an entire war. Now Mama was finally happy, and she began to learn to let me go. But it would be hard. We'd been through so much, and bonded I suppose in a way that other mothers and sons usually didn't. We were so closely knitted together.

Now Mama began to channel her energy into looking towards a permanent home for all of us. 'I want us to start *entirely* fresh now, Sasha!' she said one day. 'Completely new!'

'How completely new? In Poland? Nothing is new here, Mama. Most of it's just a mess.'

'Exactly! Destroyed by the war. So we must look elsewhere. We should move away from Poland. From Germany. From the *whole* of Europe!'

'What? Where?' She was sounding a little insane about it now. 'And anyway, how? We can't afford to move again.'

'I don't know yet, Sasha. But I have heard there are places we can go that do not cost much. Oh, I *do* want to leave now! I want to get away from here, start again far away from the death and destruction that we've had around us for so long.'

'But where?'

'Well, I don't know yet! But I will begin to investigate possible destinations. You are still only nineteen. You've been studying hard but there are no jobs here, Sasha. A new place will hold many more possibilities.'

I knew she was right. Possibilities not just for me, but for Mila and me together.

Over the next few months many changes occurred for us. My Aunty Binka and Alan had by now already left Europe. They'd gone to live in Israel, and were eager to start a new life there, now that Israel had been declared a sovereign nation. That had been in May last year. Before she left, Binka had promised to look after Stefanie too, now that she was an orphan of the war as well, with both Sonia and Zayda gone. I sometimes wondered how Stefanie coped with all of that, knowing how her parents died, how both Zayda and Sonia were killed in such terrible ways.

So the half-sisters, Binka and Stefanie, ended up together at last in Israel. Stefanie had met a Jewish man called Simon while she'd been crossing the border from Poland into Germany, and she'd married him not long after. Simon's brothers were already living in Palestine in the days before the State of Israel was declared, so Stefanie would have some relatives close by and was happy to go with Binka and start their new life together.

'Anything to get away from where Mama and Papa were killed and those awful memories. Anywhere... Papa would have liked to know I was going with Binka to Israel,' Stefanie said to Mama and me. I knew she was right. Zayda would have been happy.

In the meantime, Rena, Wicek and Selena had made other plans. Rena feared that because Wicek was not Jewish he wouldn't be readily accepted in Israel, so they decided not to follow Binka. Instead they wanted to go to America. I still had dreams of going there some day too. Of course Binka wanted to be with us as well, but Mama wasn't entirely sure about going to America. Mama seemed to be thinking about other places. She'd heard about another country, vast with possibilities. Many immigrants were going there, she said. Rena and Wicek had even mentioned it.

'Where, Mama? If we don't go with Binka to Israel, then –'

'Oh, I am frightened of going to Israel,' Mama continued. 'Really I am. War will break out between the Arabs and the Israelis! We have seen too much war. The region is too volatile, Sasha. I will not live near war again, not at any cost.'

'Yes, Mama, I suppose you're right.' I didn't want war again at any cost either.

'Well, we could go to America still,' I suggested. 'If Rena and Wicek aren't going to Israel and they go to America, then we could go with them.' I thought that was a good idea.

'Yes, we could...' said Mama, sounding hopeful and energised about it at last. So she began the application process for us to go to America. We started to apply and had medical tests and everything. But the medical tests showed that I had a heart murmur. I didn't even know what that was. They said it wasn't serious, just enough to make them think twice about letting me into America. My application was rejected.

Mama was desperately disappointed. She'd so strongly wanted to keep honouring the promise made to her mother: to keep her sisters together. They'd almost all survived the war in the same country. Now it looked like they'd have to be apart for the rest of their lives. But then Mama thought of another possibility...

'Australia!' Mama said suddenly one day, very excited.

'What?'

'Australia! Isn't it *exciting*? There is a city called... Melbun and...'

'Mama, are you joking?'

'Of course I am not joking.' She looked disappointed that I'd even think she was.

'Australia is accepting European refugees, Sasha. I know Rena and Wicek can't come to Australia but –'

'Why not?'

'Well, they applied to Australia before they applied for America apparently, but Wicek's application was denied, like yours for America. Something about an injury to his hand that he'd got in the war.'

It was true. Yet when I went through the same medical tests, my Australian application was accepted with no problems at all. Wicek had been rejected for Australia and I had been rejected for America. It was all so strange.

So Australia it was. That's where we would make our new life. But I still wasn't convinced...

'Australia, Mama? Really? But it's so far away.'

'Think of the opportunities, Sasha. And the space. It is such a *huge* country.'

'It says in my geography book that it's mainly desert.'

'No, Sasha. There are cities. Proper cities. We can go to... Melbun.'

'Melbun?'

'Well, I think that's how it is pronounced . . .'

'I don't know, Mama. We don't know anyone in Australia.' I was thinking about Mila and wondered where she was going.

'Sasha, we hardly know anyone here! Everyone's been displaced by the war. Or killed. And you will have a good education in Australia and space to play football, and horses! Remember what you said once? That you'd like to ride a horse? Well then, they have horses in Australia, lots of horses.'

'Mama . . .'

'Sasha, I have to look out for us. America and Israel are out.'

We talked some more about Australia that day, but I wasn't really enthusiastic, not like Mama was. I liked the idea of football and horses, but it was so far away. If I didn't like it there . . . I didn't know if I could come back. And what about Mila?

But the decision had been made. And when Mama made up her mind, that was pretty much it. The applications had been completed. We were going to Australia.

Before leaving Europe, though, there were so many things we had to do. More practical things to worry about than horses and football. We had to be immunised for one thing. I got my shots in Feldafing the following week, but I had a bad reaction and I had to stay with Aunty Rena for a few days to recuperate. Mama came from Munich to see me and when she walked into the room she was startled to find a girl sitting by my bedside holding my hand. Mama hadn't known about me and Mila. She'd always been away with Misha when Mila had visited me in Munich, and she'd seen her occasionally at Feldafing but never with me.

'Mama, you remember Mila, don't you?'

Mama pursed her lips. 'I am not sure I do. Hello, Mila,' she said, eyeing her suspiciously.

'Hello, Mrs Fein. It's so nice to meet you,' Mila smiled.

Mama stared at her. I was starting to feel uncomfortable. Aunty Rena had mentioned Mila sometimes, but I think Mama just thought that she was a friend, nothing more. But now, seeing Mila holding my hand like that, it was clear to Mama that something was going on.

Mila began to sense that things were uncomfortable too. She stood up and said, 'Well, I should leave the two of you to catch up. I'm sure you have a lot to talk about!' She kissed me on the cheek. 'Goodbye, Mrs Fein. I'm sure I will see you again soon.'

'Goodbye,' said Mama frostily, and I watched as Mila left to go back to her rooms.

As soon as Mila was out the door, Mama turned to me. 'And so how are you such good friends with Mila then?'

'She's just a special friend, Mama. Stop getting worried.'

'I am not worried.' She pursed her lips. 'What kind of special friend?'

'Special. Just that.' I crossed my arms then, not wanting to get into an argument. Mama was being stubborn again. But she wouldn't let the subject go. 'Well, how *long* have you been . . . "friends"?'

'Mama, you know from Aunty Rena that I met her here. I've been seeing her a fair bit.'

'A *fair bit*?'

'Well, most of the year.'

'Most of the *year*?' Mama suddenly went from trying to sound calm and matter-of-fact to being very interested indeed. So I told her a few more details, nothing too involved, and tried to change the subject. I think Mama eventually decided that this 'thing' I had with Mila would maybe fizzle out of its own accord.

'Well, my dear, I'm glad you're looking much better. Because we have a lot to get organised.'

I was glad she'd decided to follow my lead and change the subject. She continued very brightly. 'We'll be going to Melbourne very soon. It is so exciting! But I have to pack up the flat, and our ship sails in a fortnight, and you need to come home now and get your things in order.'

'Yes, I will, Mama. I'll be home soon.' I was about to tell her that Mila was travelling to Melbourne on the same ship as us, but Mama didn't need to know that yet. She'd know once we were on board.

But despite Mama's desire to leave the memories of the war behind, I knew she had mixed feelings about immigrating, especially to a country so far away. She was just like me in the end. Everything was familiar here. Her roots were here, all the memories of her beloved mother and her family life. Poland had been her home for her whole existence and it was only when she'd been displaced by war that she'd even thought about 'home' being anywhere else. Still, there was a large part of her that was relieved to leave war-torn Europe and start a new life in a place that seemed so safe, way on the other side of the world.

And so over the next two weeks Mama and I packed up our flat, finalised papers and prepared to leave Europe for a new and unknown land. Mila and her family were doing the same. I couldn't believe my luck that Mila and her family chose Melbourne as their future home too. Everyone was busy.

Everyone was thinking of what it might be like to live in a new place, with new people from all over the world.

We had no idea what to expect.

Chapter 21
COMING HOME

We travelled overland from Munich into Italy, to Genoa via Milan. There we boarded the ship the *Surriento* in February of the following year – 1950. A new decade. We were beginning again, along with many, many others leaving Europe for the very first time. I could begin to be me again.

The day we set sail was almost surreal – the smell of the shipping oil, the taste of the salt in the air and the seagulls' constant screeching and hovering above us. I clutched the railings, with Mama standing next to me, and we looked down at the ocean swirling green and grey beneath us, the salt gritty on the railings underneath our fingers. There were many Italians on our ship, whole families and lots of children running along the promenade deck, mothers trying to organise them and fathers grabbing hands and people crowding together up the gangplank and onto the ship that would take them to a new life. People were leaning over the side and waving or laughing; some were crying and hugging their friends and relatives. Others looked just plain confused.

It would take us a month to reach Melbourne. I'd looked it up in one of my books on geography. I'd read as much as I could about Australia before we left, even in school when I was supposed to be reading other things. We were going down to the bottom of the world, across a vast ocean, to the southern edge of a huge island continent. I couldn't believe we were going that far, or that such a place would be my future, and Mila's too.

There was only one immediate problem about the journey. Mila and her family knew that Mama and I were on board the same ship, but Mama didn't know that Mila was. And ships are pretty small – it's hard to avoid seeing the same people over and over again. I looked around and thought I might see Mila coming on board, up the gangplank, but there were so many crowds, mostly speaking Italian. There were a few Poles and some Germans too, but mostly there seemed to be Italians, Greeks and a few Maltese.

It was Rischek, Mila's sister's husband, who spotted us first. As soon as he could get clear of the crowds he came over to us, immensely excited and beaming a huge, broad smile.

'Sasha! Our journey begins! Look, our cabins are to have six men each, same for the women's cabins. So we should bunk together, yes? What an adventure!' he said eagerly, smiling.

'Yes, good idea. And Misha too – he could bunk with us. And Mama and Mila together.'

'Great! Well, the ladies are waiting for me to organise things. Same as usual. Some things don't change no matter which country you're in, eh, Sasha? I'll arrange everything. Leave it to me.' Suddenly Rischek was off, pushing through the crowds to see what he could do.

'Sasha, who was that?' Mama said. She hadn't met Mila's sister or Rischek.

'A friend,' I said, and was relieved when Mama didn't ask me any more, though I thought it was strange that she was smiling all of a sudden.

I nodded at Rischek, but I wasn't sure that the idea was a good one – Mila and Mama in one cabin? I was nervous about Mama with Mila when I was not there to help get Mama used to the idea that I was serious about Mila. But then Mila would have her mother and sister with her too, and the ladies would really only be in the cabin to sleep. Maybe it would give them all an opportunity to get to know each other. But maybe I should try and prepare Mama. Maybe I should tell her now . . . I just wasn't sure what to do.

I looked over the railing back towards the gangplank. There was a lot of commotion, and still many families coming on board. People scurried to and fro, eager to find their cabins and settle in.

I saw Misha with Rischek then, further down the promenade deck. That was odd. Did they know each other already? They seemed to be talking and looked pleased about something. In fact they were laughing and pointing at me. I didn't like the look of this... maybe I should just tell Mama about Mila now.

But before I had a chance to say anything, Mama looked over at Misha and smiled. 'Well, Sasha, I believe you are bunking with Misha and Rischek, and I will be in with Mila and her family. How nice that will be!'

I couldn't believe Mama knew. I didn't know how to answer. But Mama just took my hand and squeezed it tight like she used to and said, 'Don't worry, Sasha. I wasn't born yesterday, you know. I've had a lovely chat or two with Mila over the last week. I am looking forward to getting to know her more on the voyage.'

'Oh, well... I was going to tell you of course...' I began.

But Mama had been a step or two ahead of me all along. She'd spoken to Aunty Rena as they were preparing for America and while we were packing for Australia. She'd got all the details about Mila and me and knew I was attached to her. Mama thought I was too young – that's what worried her, but she decided in the end not to fight it. She'd spoken to Mila and her family before we'd even sailed, without giving away a thing to me and everyone was very happy. She'd get to know Mila more, and see what happened.

On the voyage out through the Mediterranean and towards the Suez Canal, our two families began the process of getting to know each other. We sat at the same table in the large dining room for all our meals; the smell of the fresh oranges on the table and the large jugs of water are strange details to remember, but that's what I recall from those first family dinners. Mama was unfailingly polite, making conversation with Mila whenever she could above the noise of the other families, many speaking Italian very loudly almost all the time. Mama could see that Mila was a lovely girl, attached to her family and now attached to me, her only son, the son she'd spent an almost solitary existence with all through the days of the war.

Mama spent most of her time with Misha and left us alone for much of the voyage. And Mila and I spent most of our time together, away from our families, sunbathing on deck, playing board games or deck quoits, or learning to dance together amongst the crowds and crowds of Greeks dancing frantically to their own special music in the ballroom at night.

The voyage through the canal and into the Indian Ocean was pretty boring really, nothing much to see except the occasional flying fish and albatross, and sometimes another passenger liner in the distance going back towards Europe. But then the weather began to get noticeably warmer, until finally one day, a starkly bright summer's day in 1950, the *Surriento* dropped her anchor under the scorching Australian sun.

Like so many other ships from Europe, the *Surriento*'s first port of call was Fremantle, Western Australia. We were still a long way from Melbourne.

We came on deck to watch as we berthed at the docks, people waving and excited, relieved too that the crossing of the Indian Ocean was complete. Crowds jostled once more, a garble of different languages. Sometimes some words in Polish could be heard, and some talked about Fremantle Harbour during the war, which had been home to American, British and Dutch submarines: strange to think that the war had even touched a place so far away as this.

But after only a few minutes the heat and the noise of the crowds started to get to me, and I returned to our cabin to lie on my bunk, in the cool of the lower decks. I was happy to leave Mila and everyone up there, and be quiet by myself for a while. In truth I was a bit overwhelmed by seeing my new country, how hot it looked, how dry the hills in the distance, how far away from home I was.

My bunk was just below the waterline, and I could see the grey-green water lap against our one porthole. I tried to sleep, but only dozed, and I could hear all the commotion outside on the upper decks, with people hurrying around: I suppose they really wanted to see their new country. Not me, though. Not now.

I lay there and thought back to home, to Poland and my beautiful town of Lwów. There were times when I couldn't even tell if I was dreaming or if I was awake. I remember so many things. Especially the one day that haunts me still, the day Mama and I were hiding in the barn, and I heard the shots, and terrible cries outside.

I thought of the bombs, the explosions, the day the Ukrainians came to our home, the cries of the men, women and children. I thought of what I'd seen from my bedroom window, the day the Nazis came to town.

It all seemed so long ago now, and yet there I was again, a frightened boy, crying and yelling at Mama. 'I can't do it! You want too much from me, Mama!' My heart thumped harder just thinking about it. I had been only thirteen then, and so confused.

How do you try and forget things that change your life forever? Can you? Can you ever forget?

I don't think you can. Or should. Now I thought of all the details of our apartment in Lwów, the walnut timber bedheads, the tiny details on the plasterwork round the ceiling. I remembered sobbing for ages the day I had to wear that dress for the first time. I stood in front of a mirror and looked at myself, dressed as a girl. The dress that saved my life.

Then I imagined again the sound of bombs dropping, the sound of the Ukrainian boots thumping up the stairs and suddenly I was fully awake again because Mama had come down to the cabin to get me.

'You were thinking again, weren't you?' she said.

'Yes. Just daydreaming.'

'About?'

'Home. Just home.'

'But darling, out *there* is home now.' She pointed to the porthole and the waves lapping at the edges. 'Your new country, *our* new country. Australia! It will be all right, you'll see. Come on up and join the others. Come and see Mila. She is waiting for you.'

So I did as Mama said and went back up outside. But all the time I couldn't help thinking about *me*, standing in front of that mirror. It was then that a faint thought occurred to me, for the very first time, just a glimmer in the back on my mind.

There was something I had to do.

Mama, Mila and I – all of us – disembarked in Fremantle to have a first look around on Australian soil. The sun was fierce and we thought we should try and find a cafe or somewhere where we could all have a cool drink.

We found the local hotel, but Mama was shocked to discover that the ladies had to go into a separate room from the men. 'What a ridiculous custom,' said Mama, aghast. 'I have *never* heard of such a thing!' Lots of this was going to be new to us, I thought. New customs, new ways of doing things. We were, after all, immigrants now: this was entirely different from the hotels in Europe, where men and women could drink together. I wondered what else we'd find that would be utterly strange to us.

When we returned to the ship, Mila and I could relax a little more, away from the heat and the crowds, so we found a spot in the shade on the promenade deck and sat in deckchairs reading. Mila was absorbed in a novel, but I'd started to read about Melbourne, our new home. Not so far away now, I thought, as I looked at a map in my book.

'Mila, did you know that a hundred years ago gold was discovered in Victoria? At places called Ballarat and Bendigo.' The names sounded so foreign to my ears. I didn't know how to pronounce them, and could only guess. 'They're about a hundred miles or so from Melbourne. It says here that people came from Britain, Ireland and China to search for gold. That's why they called Melbourne "Marvellous Melbourne". And business really boomed during the gold rush. It sounds like a very wealthy city. A good place for us to go, Mila.'

Mila looked up from her book. She was pleased to see me so animated about something. It was true – I *was* excited. Now I had an entirely new prospect ahead of me. Ahead of us. Together. We would live in Melbourne. A boom town. The place where we would begin again.

But there was something else too – something I'd only just worked out. Just then, as I was reading and as I watched Mila read her story. That's what it was, that faint glimmer I'd had as I lay in my bunk. This past of mine – I had to tell it. I suddenly realised that I would have to tell this story, of the boy who became a girl. I'd have to tell how I'd survived this terrible thing they were now beginning to call the Shoah, a Holocaust of humanity. I would have to write it down because others couldn't, others like Sam and Walter, like Zayda and Sonia, and Mania, and countless others who had not survived such terrible, unthinkable things. I had to write it down, or give it to someone else to write down at the very least. I was no writer, I knew that, but perhaps someone in my family would be, if I could just tell them.

However I did it, I knew there and then, before I'd even arrived in Melbourne, that one day my story about the boy who became a girl would be told.

'Look, Mila,' I said, pointing enthusiastically to a picture in my book. 'There is a touch of Europe in Melbourne,' and I showed her a picture of a cathedral called St Paul's, and another called St Patrick's. 'The architecture is so beautiful. And, look, there is even a wonderful synagogue in a place called South Yarra. I am sure we will like it there, Mila. It will be our new home.'

I was truly excited now to see something so familiar. The buildings reminded me very much of home. But it wasn't just these things that were making me happy right now. I had Mila, and Mama, and our families, and I had a story to tell.

I closed my book and took Mila's hand in mine.

THE STORY BEHIND THE STORY

My father and grandmother and the rest of my family lived in Melbourne for the remainder of their lives. In time, when her English improved and she could apply the skills acquired in her youth, my grandmother, Larissa, landed a plum secretarial job.

Misha died of a heart attack some years after my birth and Larissa married for a third time, yet was widowed again. However, in her twilight years, she met her intellectual match when a former journalist walked into her life and became her companion until her death in 1994.

My beloved father, Sasha, left his office work when he was about forty and turned to real estate. He became successful, providing a modest, but secure income for him and Mila. In his spare time, he wrote short stories, a play, poetry and a new love was born.

Sadly, my dear father died in 2006. He was taken from us too soon. And in 2017, my dear mother Mila also passed away.

This story, told here by Sasha himself, is based upon the memoir of my grandmother, Larissa. The memoir is all the more remarkable because it was written in English, even though Polish was Larissa's native tongue. She knew her story had to reach as many people in the world as possible. The names were changed at my mother's request as she had felt it was the family's personal story and lived experience. Since her passing, I feel the need to acknowledge that it was my family's story. This is for Larissa and Sasha.

My grandmother will never read this version of her extraordinary life. She passed away in Melbourne in 1994. I loved her dearly and in some ways I do think she looked upon me as the girl she never had. Before she died, she asked me to write the story of how she and her only child Sasha survived the Holocaust. I promised Larissa that I would do this, and see that it was published. Larissa wanted the world to know how she and Sasha lived through and survived one of the darkest times in human history. She wanted her story to inform readers of the horrors inflicted by the Nazi dictatorship, of the barbarity and inhumanity of Adolf Hitler, of what can happen when people forget their humanity.

In 1945, trials were held in Nuremberg, Germany, where surviving Nazis were tried for war crimes – crimes against humanity. Germany made payments to many Jewish Holocaust survivors, and to Israel for the persecution of Jews during the Holocaust and as compensation for Jewish property stolen by the Nazis. In Europe where terror once reigned, memorials and museums have been created and former concentration camps have been preserved to remember the Holocaust and the millions of its victims.

So my grandmother's and my father's story commemorates those lives lost and those who suffered in that dark,

dark period in our history. Such stories need to be kept alive. We must secure a peaceful world in the present and a peaceful future for all our children, everywhere. To do this, we must all remember our common humanity.

How did we come by Sasha's story in the first place? Many years ago now, Sasha had written a short story about how he survived the Holocaust dressed as a girl. The story was more factual than personal, focusing on the events of the war and how he assumed a female identity. Sasha wanted this story published. But the magazine he sent it to didn't accept his piece for publication. And so he shrugged the rejection off good-naturedly and returned the piece to his drawer. There it lay, for many years, until one day he showed it to me.

Sasha didn't really want to talk much about the war. He wanted to forget it. But he did say one thing to me. He said, 'Each day that I was alive after the events of the war was a bonus, for I should have died in the Holocaust. Instead, I was one of the lucky ones. I rebuilt my life with Mila, in Melbourne, and together we could move on.'

Forever jovial and jolly, Sasha was an eminently optimistic man – warmly grinning, intelligent and loving. Always with a joke up his sleeve, he was a wonderful father who was joyous upon the birth of his three grandchildren. He was a 'hands on' doting grandpa.

Larissa, bold, courageous and outspoken to the end, kept abreast of the news across the globe. She was a loving, warm Nanna and shared a special bond with her family.

With Larissa there was always a lingering sadness in her eyes. Unlike Sasha, she did talk to me about his female identity during the war. But she didn't delve into what it meant for him. All she said was this: 'You know, Sasha lived as a girl.'

I didn't ever think to ask Sasha to describe how he actually felt living as a girl or how he kept going with that extraordinary deception? I could see he'd put it behind him, yet I now regret that I hadn't asked him those questions. I had to imagine those feelings an adolescent boy would have had.

In 1994, quite unexpectedly, Larissa handed me her memoir. It was written in English, handwritten in blue ink on loose-leaf paper. 'This is for you,' she said. 'And since you are now becoming a writer, please, you must tell this story for us.' She handed me the bundle of papers, including Sasha's story that had been tucked away in that drawer all those years. I stared at it, numb. This was a huge responsibility. But I promised her. I promised that I'd do my best to write and publish the story of Sasha and Larissa.

At first, I couldn't even look at the pile of papers. So I placed the memoir inside my desk drawer, and there it lay – for twenty years. A promise not broken, but not fulfilled either. I had been busy rearing my children and writing my other books.

Twenty years later, something compelled me to take out that bunch of paper from the drawer and read it. I felt able to revive the tale of Sasha and the girl once more. When I did, I was blown away. Blown away by this messy, fragmented story that moved from past to present, hovering backwards and forwards from place to place and detail to detail. But it was this that formed the basis of Sasha's story as it is recorded here. I have simply filled in the gaps where it was needed.

And so here we have it. The life of Sasha and Larissa before, during and after the war, blending the personal with the political, the intimate with the global landscape of war. Never to forget.

Anita Selzer

TIMELINE

17 November 1929   Sasha is born in Schwabendorf, outside Brody, Poland.

1931   Pogroms occur in Lwów, Poland.

1933   Sasha and Larissa move to Lwów.

1933   Dachau, the first concentration camp in Germany, is founded.

1933–1938   Anti-Semitic laws are enacted in pre-war Germany.

1937   Measures are taken to limit Jews in the professions in Poland. Jews are banned from areas of public life.

9 November 1938   *Kristallnacht* – the Night of Broken Glass in Germany and Austria.

1 September 1939   Germany attacks Poland. Days later, Britain and France declare war on Germany. Germany bombs Lwów railway station.

22 September 1939   Soviets occupy Lwów.

June 1941   Germany invades and occupies Lwów. A ghetto and Judenrat (Jewish Council) are established in Lwów. Soon after, Larissa, Sasha, Binka and Rena go to Schwabendorf to Zayda. Mania and Selena are already there. They learn that Larissa's brother Daniel, an army officer, has been killed.

September 1941   Janowska camp in Lwów is established, initially as forced labour, then from March 1942 as a transit camp during mass deportations to concentration camps. By mid 1943 it is transformed into an extermination camp.

8 December 1941   The United States of America join the war.

1942   Sasha and Larissa return to Lwów to see a doctor due to his ear infection. After his recovery, they return to Schwabendorf. In 1942, the Nazis opened the extermination camps of Treblinka, Sobibor and Belzec for Polish Jews. Zayda is beaten to death in Belzec concentration camp. Sasha's paternal grandparents are arrested.

Sasha and Larissa assume false identity papers. Sasha becomes Sala. They return to Lwów. Binka remains in Brody, but soon returns to Larissa in Lwów. Rena and Wicek look after Selena in Lwów.

Ukrainian police interrogate Sasha alone in the apartment.

1943   Larissa joins Zegota to work with Bella. Bella informs Larissa of the Ravensbruck concentration camp. In June, the Germans liquidated the remains of the Lwów ghetto.

July 1944   Lwów is liberated from Nazi control as Polish and Soviet armies rise up together against the Nazis. Larissa learns of the death of her sister Mania. Sasha readjusts to being male.

1945   Sasha, Larissa and Wicek go to Warsaw to search for Bella. Larissa and Sasha move to Gliwice, on the border between Poland and Germany, to start a new life. Sasha meets Adriana.

7 May 1945   Germany surrenders unconditionally to the Allies.

1947   Sasha and Larissa go to Pocking Displaced Persons Camp, in the US zone of Germany, near the Austrian border. They relocate to Munich afterwards, where Sasha goes to study. Larissa meets Misha, her future husband.

Sasha meets Mila, his future wife, in Feldafing Displaced Persons Camp.

1950   Sasha and Larissa and Misha arrive in Melbourne, Australia, with Mila and her family after their journey together on the *Surriento* from Europe. A little earlier, Binka and Alan, Stefanie and Simon go to Israel. Rena, Wicek and Selena go to America.

GLOSSARY

aktion Nazi capture of Jews to send them to concentration camps

anti-Semitism hatred towards Jews

Armia Krajowa Home Army, the dominant Polish resistance movement in Nazi-occupied Poland

Art Nouveau international style of architecture and the arts, 1890–1910

Aryan according to Hitler, non-Jewish, tall blue-eyed blondes of Nordic stock

Auschwitz-Birkenau a concentration camp in Poland

bubbe grandmother

challah traditional braided Jewish bread made of flour, eggs, yeast oil and sugar

depression unemployment, low production, low levels of trade and investment

Einzatsgruppen mobile Nazi killing units

Gestapo brutal German State Secret Police

Haskalah philosopher Moses Mendelssohn's Jewish

Enlightenment championing secularisation, good relations between Jews and Christians, and religious tolerance

illegitimate   a child born out of wedlock

Judenrat   a Council representing the Jewish community in German-occupied territory during World War Two

Lebensraum   living space; Nazi policy in World War Two to conquer parts of Europe for Germany

Nazi concentration camp   a camp in which people were imprisoned, malnourished, cruelly treated, forced to work hard and eventually exterminated

Panzer   a German armoured unit – a tank

Passover   a Jewish festival celebrating the liberation of Jews from slavery in Egypt under the leadership of Moses

Red Army   Soviet Army created by the Communist government in Russia after the Bolshevik Revolution of 1917

pogrom   an organised massacre of Jews

Sabbath   Friday evening to Saturday evening as a day of rest and worship

SA Brownshirts   Storm Troopers in the Nazi Party, a violent paramilitary organisation

SS Hitler's special forces carrying out mass killings of civilians and overseeing Nazi concentration camps

Wehrmacht unified armed forces of Germany: the army, navy and air force

***Yiddishkeit** Jewish way of life

zayda grandfather

zloty Polish currency

Zegota Polish underground resistance movement

ACKNOWLEDGEMENTS

I would like to thank the Penguin team for the production of this book. I am very grateful to Bob Sessions, former publishing director of Penguin Books and now publishing consultant, who has become a friend, for his advice and belief in the need for this story to be published. Gratitude is extended to publisher Lisa Riley and commissioning editor Amy Thomas for their unstinted enthusiasm in publishing *I am Sasha*. Thanks to Amy Thomas for her meticulous editing and making my writing journey joyous. I am also indebted to Suzanne Wilson for working on the manuscript so excitedly with me and in such a masterly way.

A special thank you to Penguin Random House designer Tony Palmer for his ingenious design of the front cover and rest of the book.

Appreciation is extended to Penguin Random House publicity manager, Tina Gumnior, and rights manager, Eleanor Shorne-Holden, for all their hard work in circulating the book.

A heartfelt thanks is extended to my family and friends, for their unwavering support.

ABOUT THE AUTHOR

Anita Selzer writes non-fiction for children and adults. Her interest is in women and history. She has written about Australian sportswomen who achieved at high levels including the Olympics: athletes, basketballers, golfers, hockey players, netballers and swimmers; girls' education in Australia; governors' wives in Australia; and the pastoral pioneers of Como House. Before becoming a writer, Anita was a teacher of English and Politics and completed Masters and Doctorate degrees in Education, focusing on gender and history. She also has a Graduate Diploma in Women's Studies.

Anita is married with three children and lives in Melbourne.